NTP SECURITY

A QUICK-START GUIDE

Allan Liska

Apress®

NTP Security: A Quick-Start Guide

Allan Liska
Herndon, Virginia, USA

ISBN-13 (pbk): 978-1-4842-2411-3   ISBN-13 (electronic): 978-1-4842-2412-0
DOI 10.1007/978-1-4842-2412-0

Library of Congress Control Number: 2016961804

Managing Director: Welmoed Spahr
Acquisitions Editor: Susan McDermott
Developmental Editor: Laura Berendson
Technical Reviewer: Melissa Kelley
Editorial Board: Steve Anglin, Pramila Balen, Laura Berendson, Aaron Black,
    Louise Corrigan, Jonathan Gennick, Robert Hutchinson, Celestin Suresh John,
    Nikhil Karkal, James Markham, Susan McDermott, Matthew Moodie,
    Natalie Pao, Gwenan Spearing
Coordinating Editor: Rita Fernando
Copy Editor: Lauren Marten Parker
Compositor: SPi Global
Indexer: SPi Global
Cover Image: Designed by Olga_spb - Freepik.com

Distributed to the book trade worldwide by Springer Science+Business Media New York, 233 Spring Street, 6th Floor, New York, NY 10013. Phone 1-800-SPRINGER, fax (201) 348-4505, e-mail orders-ny@springer-sbm.com, or visit www.springer.com. Apress Media, LLC is a California LLC and the sole member (owner) is Springer Science + Business Media Finance Inc (SSBM Finance Inc). SSBM Finance Inc is a Delaware corporation.

For information on translations, please e-mail rights@apress.com, or visit www.apress.com.

Apress and friends of ED books may be purchased in bulk for academic, corporate, or promotional use. eBook versions and licenses are also available for most titles. For more information, reference our Special Bulk Sales–eBook Licensing web page at www.apress.com/bulk-sales.

Any source code or other supplementary materials referenced by the author in this text is available to readers at www.apress.com. For detailed information about how to locate your book's source code, go to www.apress.com/source-code/.

Printed on acid-free paper

Apress Business: The Unbiased Source of Business Information

Apress business books provide essential information and practical advice, each written for practitioners by recognized experts. Busy managers and professionals in all areas of the business world—and at all levels of technical sophistication—look to our books for the actionable ideas and tools they need to solve problems, update and enhance their professional skills, make their work lives easier, and capitalize on opportunity.

Whatever the topic on the business spectrum—entrepreneurship, finance, sales, marketing, management, regulation, information technology, among others—Apress has been praised for providing the objective information and unbiased advice you need to excel in your daily work life. Our authors have no axes to grind; they understand they have one job only—to deliver up-to-date, accurate information simply, concisely, and with deep insight that addresses the real needs of our readers.

It is increasingly hard to find information—whether in the news media, on the Internet, and now all too often in books—that is even-handed and has your best interests at heart. We therefore hope that you enjoy this book, which has been carefully crafted to meet our standards of quality and unbiased coverage.

We are always interested in your feedback or ideas for new titles. Perhaps you'd even like to write a book yourself. Whatever the case, reach out to us at editorial@apress.com and an editor will respond swiftly. Incidentally, at the back of this book, you will find a list of useful related titles. Please visit us at www.apress.com to sign up for newsletters and discounts on future purchases.

—*The Apress Business Team*

For Dr. Robert Bornmann. Thank you for your service and for welcoming us into your family.

Contents

About the Author

Allan Liska is an intelligence architect at Recorded Future. Allan has more than 15 years' experience in the world of security and has worked as both a security practitioner and an ethical hacker. Through his work at Symantec, iSIGHT Partners, FireEye, and Recorded Future, Allan has helped countless organizations improve their security posture using more effective intelligence. He is the author of *The Practice of Network Security* and *Building an Intelligence-Led Security Program* and the coauthor of *DNS Security: Defending the Domain Name System* and *Ransomware: Defending Against Digital Extortion*.

About the Technical Reviewer

Melissa Kelley is a software engineer living in Lawrence, Kansas. Her experience includes system administration and 15 years of software development, specializing in Java web applications. Melissa currently writes distributed marketing management software for Brandmuscle in Kansas City, Missouri. She earned a B.S. in Mathematics from the University of Kansas.

Melissa spends her free time tinkering with electronics, programming Minecraft mods for her two kids, and cooking. She is currently working on programming her house.

Acknowledgments

Any time you write a book like this, there are so many people to thank that it is hard to keep track of everyone. There are definitely some people at the top of my list. I have to start with Rita Fernando and Susan McDermott, first for believing in the book, and secondly for pushing me to stay on track, especially as I fell behind. I also need to thank my technical editor, Melissa Kelley. Thank you for double checking my work and diving deep into the sources I referenced to make sure I got things right, especially after late nights of writing.

I also want to thank all of the people who have worked so hard to build and maintain the NTP codebase for more than 30 years! At the top of that list has to be Dr. David L. Mills for his stewardship of the protocol and the code that will forever bear his stamp. But there are many other people, like Harlan Sten, Juergen Perlinger, Dr. Stephen Bellovin, and everyone at the Network Time Foundation.

I also want to thank all of the security researchers out there that help to make NTP, and other hidden programs that hold the Internet together, more secure. It is often a thankless job, but one that is necessary. It is also a job that keeps everyone protected.

Finally, I need to thank Kris and Bruce. Another book means another few months of me locked away researching and writing, and less time to spend with you. Thank you, as always, for being so understanding. I love you.

Introduction

In December of 2013, I was a sales engineer at Symantec. It was the week before Christmas, and it was very quiet. With no meetings and no training, I spent time doing what I normally did with my down time: playing around with the data stream coming in from our honeypots, looking for something interesting.

It turned out there was something very interesting going on: a huge spike in NTP traffic. I was curious as to what was going on. It turned out that hackers had discovered the monlist command in NTP. Monlist is a command that outputs a whole lot of data, but only takes a little bit of data to issue a query. That makes it perfect for use in Distributed Denial of Service (DDoS) attacks. Eventually, hacker groups went on to launch what was at that time the largest DDoS attack in history.

The thing was, security researchers and the NTP developers had known about this potential attack and had issued security recommendations to prevent these types of attacks from occurring. But no one saw them.

Even today, more than three years later, there are still unpatched public-facing NTP servers that can be used in these types of attacks. The reason for this is that NTP is an obscure protocol. It is critical for the functioning of the Internet, but most people don't know anything about it. They set the protocol when a new system is deployed, then they forget all about it.

That is part of the reason why I wrote this book. I want to raise awareness of NTP and the potential security risk it poses to networks if not secured properly.

Thank you for your interest in this book. I would love to hear your feedback, good and bad, about the book. If you have any comments, you can email me at allan@allan.org.

Understanding NTP

Marking the passage of time has played a role in every great civilization, and as civilizations have continued to evolve, they have also developed a need for more precise timekeeping. The Sumerians, in early Mesopotamia, were content to track the months and years—as early as 3500 BCE—while the Egyptians, a few centuries later, used giant obelisks to track the time during the day. Even within civilizations, the marking of time continued to advance. The Egyptians moved from obelisks to more precise and portable sundials that divided days into 12 parts and were used to track working hours. Shadow clocks allowed Egyptians to track time day and night, and water clocks were used to track time irrespective of the sun.

Other civilizations built on the idea of the water clock and refined it to the point that the Romans used water clocks as alarm clocks and the Greeks used them as stopwatches. Refinements on the water clock continued through the 13th century, when the mechanical clock was introduced.

A mechanical clock is different than a water clock, even if the water clock relies heavily on gears, as those in the 13th century did. A mechanical clock is different because it has an escapement. An escapement is a mechanical device that releases a small amount of energy over a fixed period of time, resulting in the movement of, in the case of a clock, gears, which in turn move the hands on a clock. The earliest mechanical clock was a Verge and Foliot Escapement, which used a regulating weight attached to a cord that was wrapped around a drum. The tension from the weight falling slowly turned the drum, which caused the crown gear to turn, which in turn moved the pinion, and the hands on the clock turned.

© Allan Liska 2016
A. Liska, *NTP Security*, DOI 10.1007/978-1-4842-2412-0_1

Like the first obelisks in Mesopotamia and Egypt, the first mechanical clocks were used in churches and town squares to mark the passing of time for the entire town.

Mechanical clocks offered an advantage over water clocks because they had less drift. Drift, in the field of horology, is the amount of time that a timekeeping device strays from the correct time over a given period. The best water clocks had a drift of about 15 minutes over the course of a day. So, if the correct time was 11:00 PM, a water clock could report the time as being anywhere from 10:45 PM to 11:00 PM. However, improvements in the technology of the underlying mechanical clocks significantly reduced drift. In fact, drift in mechanical clocks was halved roughly every 30 years, so that by the end of the 20th century drift, in an everyday mechanical clock it was only seconds a day.

In the early 19th century, the first electric clocks were introduced. The first electrical clocks were battery powered, but the DC (direct current) did not power the clock itself—instead, it powered the mechanical mechanism, which in turn powered the clock. Essentially, the batteries replaced the winding mechanism. Early DC-based electric clocks did not offer improvement in drift, but AC (alternating current) electric clocks eventually did.

AC-based electric clocks became much more pervasive as alternating current won out of direct current in the electricity battles of the late 19th and early 20th century. By the 1930s, AC-based electrical clocks were the most popular type of clocks in the United States. AC-based electric clocks offered the advantage of improved accuracy. AC-based clocks used a cycle motor, which did not impact the timing mechanism; rather, the cycle motor acted as a meter for the actuating impulse of the AC power delivered by the electric company. Most electric companies settled on a 60-hertz standard for delivering AC power, so the current alternated 60 times per second. The meter in an AC-based electric clock synchronized the time to the current to ensure the clock remained accurate and drift was kept to a minimum. Even if an AC-based electric clock did drift a couple of seconds over a period of time, it would synchronize with the cycle from the electric company to make up those seconds, thus keeping AC-based electric clocks accurate to within a few seconds per month.

The problem with timekeeping so far was that the clocks did not keep time consistently. Each one of the clocks described above was subject to drift based on environmental variables. Changes in temperature or altitude could significantly alter the amount of drift to which a clock was subject.

In the 20th century, accurate timekeeping became much more important. In a now-global world, precise timekeeping was important for communication, travel, and collaboration. To this end, in 1928 the first quartz clock was developed by Warren Morrison and Joseph Horton at Bell Telephone Laboratories (now known as Nokia Bell Labs and responsible for many inventions we take for granted today). Quartz clocks were different because they did not rely on mechanics to keep track of time; instead, the clock used a power source (usually a battery) to send an electronic signal through circuit to a quartz crystal, which would vibrate (properly known as oscillating). One of the unique properties of quartz is that it oscillates 32,768 times per second. It does this no matter where it is, or what the temperature is. The circuit counted the number of oscillations, and when it reached 32,768, it told the clock to advance one second. Quartz clocks were low-powered, so a single battery could keep it running for months or years with very little drift. A quartz clock was usually accurate to within a few seconds a month and it was portable. Everyone could now have a clock as accurate as an AC clock, but always with them.

At about the time quartz clocks were being developed, a different, even more accurate type of clock was also being developed: the atomic clock. The concept of an atomic clock was not new. It is believed that Scottish physicist James Clerk Maxwell first suggested the use of atoms as a way to measure time in the 1870s. In fact, Maxwell also suggested the idea that quartz would make an excellent oscillating material.

Building on the work of Maxwell, Isidor Isaac Rabi developed a framework for building an atomic clock in the 1930s at Columbia University. An atomic clock took the quartz clock concept and shrunk it. Instead of measuring the oscillating of a quartz crystal, the atomic clock measured the oscillation of a specific atom. The first atomic clock used the ammonia molecule as its base and was introduced in 1949. Unfortunately, ammonia was not a good choice to use in atomic clocks, and the first atomic clock was no more accurate than the best quartz clocks of the day.

In 1950, a team at the National Bureau of Standards (NBS), led by Harold Lyons and Jesse Sherwood, started development of a new atomic clock that would use cesium instead of ammonia. Cesium had a number of qualities that made it better suited as an element in an atomic clock. Unfortunately, work on the atomic clock was halted at NBS. However, in the United Kingdom there was a separate team, led by Louis Essen and Jack Perry, working an atomic clock at the National Physical Laboratory (NPL) located in Teddington.

Note NPL also broadcasts the time over the air from the Anthorn Radio Station in Cumbria, and it is known as the MSF signal. Until 2007, the signal was operated from a radio station in Rugby. The radio station has three atomic clocks, one of which is installed on site. The signal is broadcast over a frequency of 60 KHz. People all over Europe can use the signal to synchronize their clocks, but the signal spreads even farther. Researchers in Antarctica in the 1950s were able to synchronize their time by listening to the familiar "This is MSF, Rugby, England, transmitting…" every 15 minutes.

The NPL team also relied on the cesium molecule, and they released their clock in 1955. The first atomic clock was so accurate that it only had a one-second drift every 300 years. As with mechanical clocks, scientists continue to improve the accuracy of atomic clocks, so much so that today's atomic clocks have a drift of one second every 300 million years.

Quartz and atomic clocks did more than improve on the accuracy of other types of clocks; they changed the definition of time. Until the quartz clock, time was measured based on the rotation of the earth and its revolution around the sun. A second was defined as 1/86400th of a day. Because scientists now had a more accurate and consistent tool with which to measure time in 1967, a second was redefined as:

> *The second is the duration of 9,192,631,770 periods of the radiation corresponding to the transition between two hyperfine levels of the ground state of the cesium 133 atom.*[1]

Even though most people still think of time in terms of the rotation of the earth, that is no longer the case in the scientific community, and it has not been that way for decades.

While this book is not about the history of time, an understanding of how the perception of time has changed and how societies have evolved their ability to measure time is important for understanding the Network Time Protocol (NTP). A fundamental understanding of NTP is critical to understanding the security problems associated with it and how to implement NTP in the most secure way possible.

A Brief History of Time Synchronization

Almost from the invention of tools to track time, there has been a need to synchronize those tools to account for inaccuracies in measurement or flaws in the tools used to measure time.

The Sumerians were among the first civilizations to create a calendar. The Sumerian calendar followed the lunar cycle and contained 354 days divided into 12 months. Of course, since a year is actually 365.24 days long, every few years they would have to have a leap month to make up for the missing 11.24 days. This is a form of time synchronization, and allowed the Sumerians to sync their calendar with the celestial time and keep their months in the proper seasons.

---

[1]13th Conférence Générale des Poids et Mesures (CGPM) 1967/1968 Resolution 1, p 103.

Timekeeping devices eventually became smaller and even portable; it was necessary to sync them on a regular basis with permanent clocks. For many early societies, those clocks were simply the large obelisks or water clocks that remained in the center of early cities. As mechanical clocks became more common, community churches often became the authoritative "time servers." Citizens of a town or city could sync their clocks at home based on the church bells, which usually went off at the top of the hour and every fifteen minutes between the hours. The churches would ring the bells a different number of times to indicate whether it was the top of the hour, quarter of an hour, half an hour, or three quarters of an hour.

As civilizations became more interconnected, the need for synchronized time became more apparent and important. Remember that prior to the invention of the quartz and atomic clocks, time was linked to the movement of the earth and position of the sun. This meant that time between cities—even cities that were within a day's travel—could vary by minutes or hours.

When most commerce was conducted within the same city or was only conducted in an ad-hoc fashion with other cities, this time difference was not a problem. But with the rise of railroads in Great Britain, even slight variations in time could cause problems with schedules as the trains traveled from one end of Great Britain to another.

The Great Western Railway in Great Britain was the first railway to introduce *railway time*. Railway time is a way of applying a single standard time across a wide range of local times. Prior to the adoption of railway time, schedules were distributed to travelers that told them how much to adjust their watches forward/backward when they arrived in a new town. Again, this method worked perfectly fine when the primary mode of transportation was horse and buggy, but not for trains.

In 1840, the Great Western Railway decided to standardize on Greenwich Mean Time (GMT) across all of its stations. There were two reasons for this: The first is that it made it easier to track train travel across the country. The second is that the Great Western Railway had also introduced telegraph stations at some of their rail stations in 1839.

■ **Note**   Greenwich Mean Time (GMT) is equivalent to the time in London as set by the Royal Observatory, Greenwich (RGO). In 1840, the RGO was already a critical part of the fields of astronomy and naval navigation within Great Britain. The RGO was also the keeper of GMT, which was well established at the time of its introduction to the railroads and is still used today, though it has largely been superseded by Coordinated Universal Time (UTC) in the technical and scientific world.

The use of the telegraph allowed stations to sync their time to GMT. Instead of relying on offsets, paper schedules, and manual adjustments, time could now be synced almost instantaneously across the telegraph lines, directly from the RGO. GMT quickly became the standardized time across Great Britain. Initially, towns and cities were resistant to the idea of changing their clocks to match London. As the rail spread throughout Great Britain, and more railroad companies adopted GMT as their standard time, towns and cities quickly realized they need to adapt.

In the United States, the United States Naval Observatory served the same role as the RGO. Starting in 1845, the Naval Observatory managed a "time ball" that was dropped precisely at noon every day. Ships in port were able to set their clocks before heading out to sea, to ensure they would be able to maintain accurate time during their voyage. Citizens of Washington DC were also able to set watches and clocks when the time ball dropped.

The Naval Observatory eventually began using the telegraph system, which ran along railroad lines as it did in Great Britain, to synchronize time across all railroad systems.

Eventually, the telegraph was superseded by the telephone, and most telephone companies offered a time service to their customers. Anyone of a certain age will most likely remember being able to call 844- [any four numbers] and listen the message, "At the tone, the time will be…"

Note The United States Naval Observatory still maintains a phone-based time system. Calling 202-762-1401 will connect the caller to a pre-recorded message providing the time in five-second intervals.

The phone time service was important for decades because the rise of the suburbs and continued growth of the city meant that it was not easy to sync timepieces with large clock in a town square. The idea of networked clocks was not yet commonplace, so "calling time" was the only way to ensure that clocks and watches remained synchronized with the rest of the world.

The Importance of Time Synchronization in Modern Networks

Synchronizing time has always been a critical part of society. Even going back to early calendars, if the calendar drifted too far from the revolution of the earth around the sun, farmers would wind up planting crops too early or too late. As the populations of cities continued to grow, synchronizing time was important to ensure that meetings and other activities that were critical to running cities happened at the correct time. Of course, in war, time synchronization has always been important. Synchronized time allows commanders to plan attacks at specific times and coordinate troop movements against a single force or on multiple fronts. Time synchronization has also become critical in the world of finance—if time is off by even as much as a few seconds in trading systems, it can result in the loss of millions of dollars.

Beyond agrarian, military, and finance needs, as society has become more interconnected, time synchronization has become a critical part of commerce and communication.

Nowhere is this more apparent than in modern communication standards. It doesn't matter if devices are communicating over a cellular network, cable network, wireless network, or fiber optic network—time synchronization is critical to ensuring that the communication works as designed.

Each network type has its own synchronization protocol. Networked computers generally use the Network Time Protocol, but other communications networks rely heavily on synchronized timing as well. Cellular networks, for example, require phones to be properly synched to towers and to the carrier's cellular network so that calls can be properly tracked and conversations can continue uninterrupted as a phone passes from one cell tower to the next.

Each of these industries uses different standards to track time synchronization, but they all base their synchronization on the atomic clock.

The Network Time Protocol

Because accurate time on devices that communicate over the Internet is so important, early Internet pioneers realized that they needed a way to ensure those devices could synchronize time. One of the first attempts at this, outlined in Request for Comments (RFC) 868, was the Time Protocol. The Time Protocol was introduced by a team led by the great Jon Postel, and operated over either the Transmission Control Protocol (TCP) port 37 or the User Datagram Protocol (UDP) port 37. Time was delivered as the number of seconds since January 1st, 1900 00:00:00, GMT.

The protocol was relatively simple, the idea being that a node on a network could poll other systems on the same network asking for their time. The other hosts on the network that were listening on the right ports would reply with their current time as a 32-bit integer (again, expressed as seconds since January 1st, 00:00:00 GMT). If a queried host had its time set to January 1st, 2017 GMT, it would return a response of 3692217600, very similar to the way Epoch time works on UNIX systems, but with a base date of January 1st, 1900 GMT instead of a base date of January 1st, 1970 GMT.

The Time Protocol had a number of weaknesses and is not widely used today, though the *xinetd* daemon and *rdate* command still use it, as well as some cable Internet providers whose equipment supports the Time Protocol over Data Over Cable Service Interface Specifications (DOCSIS). In almost all cases, any application that requires time synchronization over a network uses NTP.

The specification for version zero of NTP was documented as part of RFC 958, written by David L Mills, in 1985. However, the roots of NTP go back further than that. The concept of time synchronization across computer connected networks was first mentioned in Internet Experiment Note (IEN) 173, "Time Synchronization in DCNET Hosts," also authored by David L Mills in February of 1981. IEN 173 became RFC 778, "DCNET Internet Clock Service," in April of 1981.

In other words, the idea of synchronizing time between computer systems across the Internet is more than 35 years old.

Understanding NTP

At its most basic, NTP is a protocol that allows network connected system clocks to synchronize time using a tiered set of distributed clients and servers. NTP allows these clocks to keep time between systems synchronized to within tens of microseconds (one second is equal to one million microseconds) of each other. It does this in a robust and scalable way without having to rely on a single centralized server that could be prone to failure.

The fact that NTP is so robust and decentralized is what has allowed to it thrive as a protocol over 35 years. It has also led to continual improvements in the protocol to allow for more accurate timekeeping and more capabilities in the underlying program.

NTP has not only continued to grow in use, but the underlying program has also been ported to a wide array of platforms, from UNIX and Linux to Microsoft Windows and Cisco's Internet Operating System (IOS) platform. In fact, almost all NTP implementations are based on the core code that is maintained by the Network Time Foundation.

While the first version of NTP left a lot of parameters undefined, the current version of NTP, version 4, is well documented in RFCs 5905 and 7822. The focus of this book is on NTPv4. Other versions of NTP have inherent and easily exploitable security flaws and should be avoided at all cost.

> **Note** Despite the fact that the NTPv4 standard was first published in June of 2010, there are still some systems that use NTPv3 as their standard. It is important to know what version of NTP is being used on systems in the network, especially closed systems, and to pressure those vendors who are still running NTPv3 to upgrade.

NTPv4 uses a hierarchical structure that allows clients to connect to one or more systems in order to sync time. There are two types of hierarchical structures inherent in NTPv4. The first is the modes of operation. In the modes of operation, a system can be a primary server, secondary server, or client. A primary server is one that is directly connected to a reference clock. A reference clock maintains time according to UTC standards. This could be one that is tied to a GPS system, an Inter-Range Instrumentation Group, or one of the other types of reference clocks.

Directly tied to the concept of modes of operation in NTP is the idea of the stratum of an NTP host. A stratum is an eight-bit integer that refers to the hierarchy of a server, loosely translated as the distance from a reference clock and a given NTP server is. Primary servers have a stratum value of 1. Secondary NTP servers have a stratum value of between 2-15 depending on its logical distance from the primary server, as well as its network path and the stability of its system clock. A stratum value of 16 means that the clock on the system is no longer synchronized with another clock.

As demonstrated in Figure 1-1, a primary NTP server with a direct connection to a reference clock is a stratum 1 server. The secondary NTP servers that sync with the primary server are stratum 2 servers. These servers not only act as clients, getting updates from the stratum 1 server, but also as servers, providing updates to stratum 3 servers or to hosts on a local network. The stratum 3 servers get updates from the stratum 2 servers and provide updates to the clients on the local network. Stratum 3 hosts can provide updates to stratum for hosts, and so on.

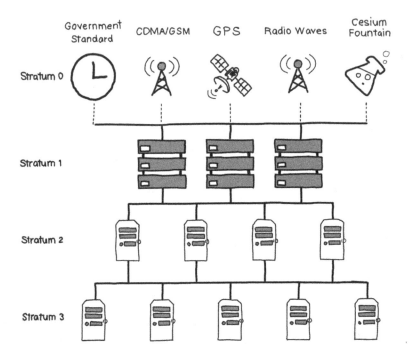

Figure 1-1. NTP Hierarchy

The only exception to this chain of updates is stratum 0, which is the stratum level reserved for the reference clocks, shown in Figure 1-1. Examples of reference time sources include GSM clocks, GPS clocks, and cesium fountain atomic clocks.

The NTP server hierarchy can exist entirely within a network, entirely external to a network, or as a hybrid of servers that reside inside and outside the network. In fact, there are several security advantages to running a stratum 1 NTP server within an organization's network. One of the primary security advantages is that it makes the organization less susceptible to NTP-based Distributed Denial of Service (DDoS) attacks, because it allows the organization to restrict access to NTP packets at the firewall. While there is undoubtedly higher cost and more complexity involved in acquiring and managing a stratum 1 NTP server, the security payoff could potentially outweigh the cost.

NTP from the Client Side

How does all this activity look from the client side? It depends on how the NTP is configured on the server side, but on the client end it is relatively simple. If a client is configured to use NTP, which most workstations are at this point, it will generally have a single domain set up that is used to sync time. That domain can point to a single host or a number of hosts.

For example, Apple workstations point to time.apple.com, which points to a number of different IP addresses depending on the location of the request, as shown in Listing 1-1.

Listing 1-1. Output of a DNS query for time.apple.com

```
server$ host time.apple.com
time.apple.com is an alias for time-osx.g.aaplimg.com.
time-osx.g.aaplimg.com has address 17.253.20.253
time-osx.g.aaplimg.com has address 17.253.20.125
time-osx.g.aaplimg.com has address 17.253.24.253
time-osx.g.aaplimg.com has address 17.253.24.125
time-osx.g.aaplimg.com has address 17.253.6.253
```

Microsoft does something similar with their workstations, which use time. windows.com, and returns a single address, as in Listing 1-2.

Listing 1-2. Output of DNS query for time.windows.com

```
server$ host time.windows.com
time.windows.com is an alias for time.microsoft.akadns.net.
time.microsoft.akadns.net has address 40.76.58.209
```

Microsoft actually recommends using the NTP servers listed at www.pool. ntp.org, or just querying 0.pool.ntp.org – 4.pool.ntp.org, which returns a series of IP addresses, just like the query to Apple and shown in Listing 1-3.

Listing 1-3. Outpoint of DNS query for 0.pool.ntp.org

```
server$ host 0.pool.ntp.org
0.pool.ntp.org has address 171.66.97.126
0.pool.ntp.org has address 216.152.240.220
0.pool.ntp.org has address 69.167.160.102
0.pool.ntp.org has address 108.61.73.243
```

▨ **Note** The use of the time.windows.com domain for time synchronization really only applies to stand-alone workstations that are not part of a domain. Microsoft Windows desktops and servers that are part of a Windows domain will synchronize time with the domain controller for that domain, unless they are instructed to do otherwise.

On the Linux side, most distributions also have their own NTP servers, some of which are managed by the team that runs pool.ntp.org, such as the servers listed in Listing 1-4 when querying ntp.ubuntu.com:

Listing 1-4. Output of DNS query for ntp.ubuntu.org

```
server$ host ntp.ubuntu.com
ntp.ubuntu.com has address 91.189.94.4
ntp.ubuntu.com has address 91.189.91.157
ntp.ubuntu.com has address 91.189.89.198
ntp.ubuntu.com has address 91.189.89.199
ntp.ubuntu.com has IPv6 address 2001:67c:1560:8003::c8
ntp.ubuntu.com has IPv6 address 2001:67c:1560:8003::c7
```

In this case, Ubuntu returns a sampling of IPv4 and IPv6 addresses in response to the query. Why do public NTP servers return multiple IP addresses in response to a single query? This has to do with the mode in which the NTP servers are configured.

NTP Server Configuration

NTP servers can be configured in a number of different ways. The most common is in a straight client-to-server configuration. This how most organizations who run their own NTP infrastructure set up their servers. In this configuration, one or more servers in the network is designated as an NTP server, and the local systems in the network point to it for synchronized time.

Generally, these are not stand-alone servers. Instead, they are web servers, mail servers, or domain controllers; they serve other functions in the organization; or they also run NTP. That is why it is a good idea to have multiple servers in the network running NTP and to configure servers and endpoints in the network to synchronize with multiple NTP servers. Even in the case of Microsoft Windows desktops, it is possible to configure a backup NTP server to the domain controller.

In the case of NTP pool servers, like pool.ntp.org or time.windows.com, the configuration is usually done using the Domain Name System (DNS) or Content Delivery Network (CDN). On the surface, the request looks like it is going to a single host—instead, that domain name masks hundreds or even thousands of servers that are constantly being rotated. This helps to distribute the load and provide the fastest response to the client. This type of DNS is really only necessary when managing hundreds of thousands to millions of NTP clients.

Another way in which an NTP server can be set up is using the anycast protocol. Anycast is a way of delivering service from multiple systems all masquerading as the same IP address. It uses a combination of special IP addressing and routing protocols—usually Border Gateway Protocol (BGP)—to deliver service in a robust manner. In the case of NTP, the NTP client would make a request to a single IP address. When the request is broadcast, even if it travels through multiple routers, it will find the closest server in that anycast configuration. The identified server will respond and answer any NTP queries. If that server crashes, or something happens to it, the next closest server will step in and respond to queries from that client, using the same IP address.

The anycast service only works with stateless protocols like NTP and DNS, which operate over UDP. Because the servers do not have to maintain any sort of state, it is easy for one server to step in when another server becomes unresponsive.

Servers and clients can also be configured in broadcast mode, though this is not done very often. Broadcast for NTP works in the same way that radio does: the NTP server sends out a signal and the clients pick it up. So, an NTP server could be configured with a line like this:

broadcast 192.168.1.255

This would send out the time periodically to all hosts on the 192.168.1.0/24 network at regular intervals. If the NTP clients on that network were configured with the broadcastclient flag, they would receive those signals automatically.

In some ways this is a more elegant solution. Instead of 254 hosts sending out queries and receiving responses, all 254 are automatically updated, so this method actually requires less back-and-forth traffic. On the other hand, if there are only 40 hosts on that Class C, it will generate even more traffic. This solution also suffers from the fact that many implementations do not support it. In fact, very few beyond the NTP reference implementation support this configuration.

NTP Reference Implementation

The NTP reference implementation is available at www.ntp.org and has been ported to dozens of different platforms and operating systems. It is referred to as the reference implementation because it includes support for every feature outlined in RFC 5905. There are other NTP programs available, but most of those don't include all the features that the reference implementation does.

The NTP program actually consists of three primary applications, as well as several others that are used less frequently. The three primary programs are:

1. ntpd – the NTP daemon itself

2. ntpdc – special NTP query program

3. ntpq – standard NTP query program

There is also the ntpdate command, which in the past has been used for one-time synchronizations. This program, while still included with most NTP packages, is deprecated, as this one-off functionality is now included in the NTP daemon.

The heart of the reference NTP implementation is ntpd, the NTP daemon. This command is used to synchronize time. It also manages the many algorithms that NTP uses to decide which of the upstream clocks to use and updates the statistics collected. All of the NTP functionality is contained within the daemon. Control of ntpd can be managed using flags upon starting up the service, or, as in most cases, it can be managed through a configuration file.

The standard naming convention for the configuration is ntp.conf, and it is normally stored in the /etc directory on most UNIX or Linux systems. A typical and basic ntp configuration file will be similar to the output shown in Listing 1-5.

Listing 1-5. *Sample ntp.conf file*

```
driftfile      /var/lib/ntp/ntp.drift
logfile        /var/log/ntp.log

server         0.ntp.pool.org        iburst
server         1.ntp.pool.org        iburst
server         2.ntp.pool.org        iburst

broadcast      192.168.1.255       minpoll 10
restrict -4    default                        noquery nomodify nopeer notrap
restrict -6    default                        noquery nomodify nopeer notrap

restrict       127.0.0.1                       nomodify nopeer notrap
restrict       192.168.1.0 mask 255.255.255.0 nomodify nopeer notrap
```

Different parts of this file will be covered throughout the book. The basics of the example include the drift file, log file, server listings, and restrict commands.

The drift file maintains information about the difference between the system clock and correct time as provided by the NTP servers. NTP implicitly trusts the NTP servers to keep more accurate time than the local clock, so it will adjust the system clock unless there is a large difference between the two times, and it records that difference. This is one of the reasons that it is recommended to synchronize with more than one server at a time. It is always possible for a single server to be off, even in a chain of NTP servers. However, it is unlikely for multiple servers in multiple chains to be off of UTC time. Synchronizing with multiple upstream servers allows NTP to calculate the time difference between the local server and all of the different upstream servers. As long as all the upstream servers agree on a time, the NTP will make any time adjustment necessary.

The log file indicates where to send NTP logs. By default, NTP will send logs to the syslog file, instead of a file specific for NTP logs. Irrespective of whether the logs are sent to syslog or to an NTP-specific file, the logs will be sent in syslog format.

The server commands are the upstream, or lower stratum, servers with which this NTP client is synchronizing. Again, the more servers the better in terms of maintaining the most accurate time and having the most redundancy. The iburst flag in the servers line instructs NTP to increase the number of queries to that server if it appears to be offline in an attempt to re-establish communication.

The restrict command will be covered in more detail in Chapter 4. It is used to limit the queries to which the NTP server will respond whether locally or from remote hosts. NTP administrators use restrict to create access control lists (ACLs) that limit interaction from remote hosts to the NTP servers.

NTP also maintains a facility for authentication. Authentication parameters are also configured in the ntp.conf file and will be discussed in the next session.

Both ntpdc and ntpq are used to communicate with the NTP daemon. They are used to pull statistics, make configuration changes on the fly, and get updates. The difference between the two is that ntpq operates using mode 6 packets, while ntpdc uses mode 7 packets. Both commands can be run interactively or from the command line, with output that looks like Listing 1-6.

Listing 1-6. Output of the sysstats command

```
allan@v623:~$ ntpq -c sysstats
uptime:                407479
sysstats reset:        407479
packets received:      2648
current version:       2588
older version:         0
bad length or format:  3
authentication failed: 0
declined:              0
restricted:            48
rate limited:          0
KoD responses:         0
processed for time:    2566
```

The sysstats command provides an overview of the packets received and processed by the NTP servers. It also shows if there have been any bad packets or failed authentication by outside hosts. There are a number of different queries that administrators can use to better understand the current state of an NTP instance, whether that is local or remote. The various commands are listed in Table 1-1.

Table 1-1. List of ntpq and ntpdc commands

List of available queries from ntpq and ntpdc			
:config	refid	mreadlist	readvar
addvars	exit	mreadvar	reslist
apeers	help	mrl	rl
associations	host	mrulist	rmvars
authenticate	hostnames	mrv	rv
authinfo	ifstats	ntpversion	saveconfig
cl	iostats	opeers	showvars
clearvars	kerninfo	passociations	sysinfo
clocklist	keyid	passwd	sysstats
clockvar	keytype	peers	timeout
config-from-file	lassociations	poll	timerstats
cooked	lopeers	pstats	version
cv	lpassociations	quit	writelist
debug	lpeers	raw	writevar
delay	monstats	readlist	

The ntpq and ntpdc commands are powerful, giving administrators great control over NTP servers. Unfortunately, they also give potential attackers great control over those servers, which is why the restrict commands are so important. They help to ensure that only those with the right access are able to issue remote commands.

NTP Authentication

Another way that NTP helps to ensure that only those who have the correct level of access are connecting to the NTP daemon is by using authentication. There are two ways to authenticate an incoming NTP request: symmetric-key encryption and AutoKey.

Symmetric-key encryption is a form of password-based authentication. Two NTP servers participating in symmetric-key encryption both use a shared key, and that key is stored on both servers. When one server sends a request to the other, it includes the key in the packet. The receiving NTP server checks the key, makes sure it matches the key stored in its key file, and proceeds with the transaction.

The NTP configuration looks like Listing 1-7 on the client side.

Listing 1-7. *Symmetric-key configuration*

```
keys /etc/ntp/keys
server [IP Address of NTP Server] key 1
trustedkey 1
controlkey 1
requestkey 1
```

The keys file is where the actual key is stored, and each key is assigned a unique number, commonly referred to as a key identifier, between 1-65535. This allows a client to connect to multiple servers using a different key for each server.

The keys file will look similar to Listing 1-8.

Listing 1-8. *NTP keys file*

```
# PLEASE DO NOT USE THE DEFAULT VALUES HERE.
#
#65535  M  akey
#1      M  pass
1 M [Password]
```

Each line has the unique key identifier, the encryption mode, and the actual password.

On the server side, the configuration is very similar, with the lines listed in Listing 1-9 added to the ntp.conf file.

Listing 1-9. *Symmetric-key encryption on the server side*

```
keys /etc/ntp/keys
trustedkey 1
controlkey 1
requestkey 1
```

A server can also maintain multiple keys. When a client connects, the request must match both the key identifier and the associated key in order to be successfully authenticated.

The other authentication scheme supported by NTP is AutoKey. AutoKey uses a private key encryption scheme for authentication. As shown in Figure 1-2, AutoKey is more complicated than symmetric encryption.

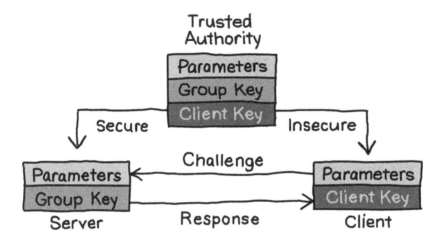

Figure 1-2. AutoKey encryption for NTP

AutoKey requires that OpenSSL be installed on the NTP host and that NTP was compiled with the –enable-autokey flag (this is the default for most packages). As Figure 1-2 shows, the primary advantage of AutoKey is that it does not require the client and server to share private keys. Instead, it relies on a trusted authority to ensure that both client and server are who they say they are. This is similar to the way that transport layer security (TLS) (more commonly known as https) transactions occur.

In addition to making changes to the ntp.conf file, AutoKey requires the use of the ntp_keygen tool to create public/private keypairs. To start, the lines shown in Listing 1-10 need to be added to the ntp.conf file.

Listing 1-10. AutoKey configuration in ntp.conf file

```
# Crypto
crypto pw [Password]
keysdir /etc/ntp
crypto randfile /dev/urandom

server [NTP server 1] autokey version 4
server [NTP server 2] autokey version 4
```

Instead of a single file, AutoKey requires a directory in which all of the keys are stored. Each server may have its own key, or one key can be used for all servers. Keys are generated using the ntp_keygen (or ntp_genkeys on older versions of NTP) and the keys are copied into the /etc/ntp directory.

The public key can be shared with clients connecting to the server, but the private key is never shared—it is simply used to verify the connection.

AutoKey is, unfortunately, not widely deployed, largely because of the complexity involved in maintaining public key infrastructure (PKI) on top of the NTP configuration. However, organizations that already have PKI in place can add AutoKey configuration to their NTP deployment relatively easily.

Mapping the Network Time Protocol

Before discussing NTP security issues, it is important to understand what NTP traffic is supposed to look like. There are two primary ways of attacking NTP: attack the daemon or attack the protocol. Unfortunately, because of the nature of NTP, attacking the protocol has been a highly successful method of attack over the years.

NTP operates over UDP port 123. UDP is a stateless and connectionless protocol. This means that everything one end of an NTP transaction needs to know about that transaction is contained in a single packet. When a client sends a request to a server, it does not know if the connection was successful or not until it gets a response. Similarly, when a server sends a response, it does not know if the client received it.

This contrasts with a TCP, which has a three-way handshake requiring confirmation of the initial connection and response.

Chapter 2 has a detailed analysis of NTP traffic, but Figure 1-3 shows the structure of an NTP packet. The top header of the packet in Figure 1-3 includes the Leap Indicator (LI), which tells the host on the receiving end whether the packet contains a leap second. It also has the version number (VN), letting the host know whether it is NTP version 0, 2, 3, or 4. It contains the mode of the packet and the stratum (0-15) of the sending host. It also contains information about how often it is polling (poll) the other host and the precision of the clock.

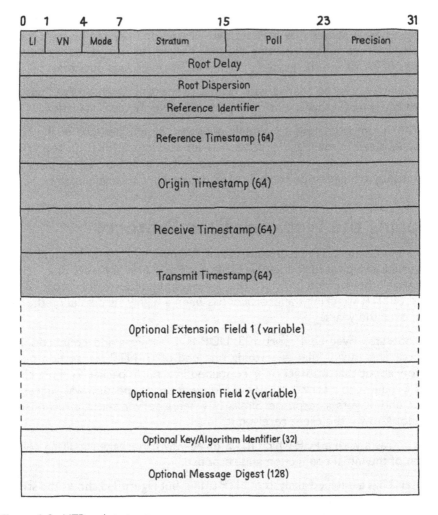

Figure 1-3. NTP packet structure

The body of the packet contains information about the time as it currently is set on the originating host, where it got that time, and what the delay and dispersion is between the time on the host and UTC (if there is any).

Understanding what a NTP packet is supposed to look like, and the type of information that is included, can help security and administrative teams troubleshoot when something is wrong.

Conclusions

Time and time synchronization has played a strong role in the development and advancement of society over tens of thousands of years. It has gotten to the point where many of society's current systems, such as transactions that occur over the web and stock market trading transactions, require the host and server to have their time closely synchronized.

This has led to the development of the Network Time Protocol. NTP is used by hosts around the world and makes use of a robust and redundant infrastructure to keep time synchronized to within nanoseconds per month.

This type of remote synchronization requires countless man hours to maintain and continue operating around the world. It also requires a reliable NTP client that servers and endpoints can use to connect to that infrastructure and trust that the time they are being given is actually correct.

The next few chapters will go into deeper detail about NTP and its potential security problems, and how to prevent those problems from creating larger problems within an organization.

Issues in NTP Security

NTP is most likely the longest continuously operating protocol on the Internet. At more than 30 years old, NTP has become pervasive across the Internet, to the point that most people don't even think about it. Unfortunately, that is part of the problem. NTP is an obscure protocol that rarely fails and does its job well. This has led to a lot of entropy in the development and deployment of the protocol.

The current version of NTP, version 4, was first introduced in 2010, and even though version 4 has been considered the standard for more than six years, there are still operating systems that don't support it. On top of that, there are a number of operating systems that don't fully implement the available security capabilities in version 4 of the protocol, opting instead to implement the Simple Network Time Protocol (SNTP). This can leave organizations open to attacks again a vulnerable NTP daemon or the organization's network vulnerable to a Distributed Denial of Service (DDoS) attack.

In a way, NTP is a victim of its own success. Because NTP just works, with almost no adjustment needed from the desktop, server, a network or security team very little attention is paid to the protocol, until something major happens.

© Allan Liska 2016

A. Liska, *NTP Security*, DOI 10.1007/978-1-4842-2412-0_2

A History of NTP Attacks

When NTP attacks happen, they tend to be big and impact large swaths of Internet-connected networks. Precisely because no one thinks about it, NTP daemons tend not to be updated and security enhancements are not always enabled. This is not something that just happens at the local network level — many vendors don't pay attention to security announcements concerning NTP.

Because NTP is an obscure protocol, and one that is not always well understood, other security concerns are prioritized over it. This can leave NTP vulnerabilities exposed for longer periods of time than other security concerns. On top of that, NTP may be given a longer patch cycle within a local network, because it is perceived as a lower risk. The time period between a vulnerability in NTP being discovered and the time it is patched at the local level can be longer than for other, more prominent protocols such as TLS or HTTP.

A great example of this is with CVE-2001-0414. CVE is the Common Vulnerabilities and Exposures database that has been maintained by The MITRE Corporation (and sponsored by US-CERT) since 1999.

■ **Note**   The CVE database is available at https://cve.mitre.org and is a very valuable resource for finding out what the latest vulnerabilities are and what systems they are impacting.

CVE-2001-0414 is a buffer overflow vulnerability in version 4.0.99k and earlier of the NTP daemon that was released in 2001. The vulnerability, if successfully exploited, would allow a remote attacker to initiate a denial of service against a system and possibly even gain remote access. The vulnerability is very serious, and was given a criticality of 10.

This was a critical vulnerability that impacted vendors across multiple platforms, including Cisco. However, it took Cisco 11 months to release a security advisory on this particular vulnerability. That means that for 11 months, Cisco routers running NTP were potentially vulnerable, to say nothing of how much longer after the security advisory was released before network administrators actually implemented the suggestions. Routers and switches tend to go long periods of time between upgrades and configuration changes, so it is not unreasonable to expect it to be at least another year before most vulnerable routers were updated.

■ **Note**   This is in no way a knock on Cisco. Cisco is normally very responsive when it comes to releasing security advisories and encouraging its customers to upgrade—this just happens to be an example of a time when they were not.

There have been a number of other NTP vulnerabilities published over the years. Some of the most critical are listed here.

CVE-2004-0657 impacted all versions of the NTP daemon prior to 4.0, and it was an integer overflow bug that would cause a server to return an incorrect date/time offset when a client requested a time that more than 34 years outside of the current time. This was a medium threat that was easy to exploit, but caused minimal damage.

CVE-2009-0159 was a buffer overflow to which all versions of NTP prior to 4.2.4p7R-C2 were vulnerable. The buffer overflow was in the cookedprint() function. The vulnerability allowed an attacker to potentially crash the NTP daemon and possibly execute a command. The cookedprint() function is part of the ntpq command subset; in fact, it is the function that is responsible for presenting NTP output in human readable format. Getting access to this type of function meant it was possible for the attacker to gain remote access to the system.

CVE-2013-5211 documented a vulnerability that was present in versions of the NTP daemon prior to 4.2.7p26, which would allow a server running the NTP service to be used in a Denial of Service (DoS) or DDoS attack. The vulnerability was with the monlist control message command, and it was not really a vulnerability as much as it was taking advantage of the way NTP works. The monlist is part of the ntp_request application that monitors the up to 600 machines that are connected to the server, along with their traffic count. The command, and its output, looks like Listing 2-1:

Listing 2-1. Output of the monlist command

```
root@server:~# ntpdc -c monlist 127.0.0.1
remote address          port local address   count m ver rstr avgint  lstint
===========================================================================
ntp-northamerica.core.   123 198.84.61.242     539 4 4    1d0    987     118
snotra.fanube.com        123 198.84.61.242     553 4 4    1d0    962     609
mail.mariocube.com       123 198.84.61.242     494 4 4    1d0   1077     673
pacific.latt.net         123 198.84.61.242     554 4 4    1d0    960     864
golem.canonical.com      123 198.84.61.242     554 4 4    1d0    960    1022
198-84-62-37.las01.rok 53197 198.84.61.242       1 3 3    1d0 185834  185834
```

Note Running the command may return the error "***Server reports data not found." This error simply means that the remote NTP server has been configured not to respond to these types of queries, which is good.

The command is a normal function of NTP, and there is nothing inherently insecure about tracking these statistics. On the other hand, the fact that this command can often be used to query remote servers, even those on different networks, is a big security risk. In fact, attackers figured out that this command could be used to launch a reflection/amplification attack. Remember, an NTP server can store up to 600 servers, along with the associated traffic information, in the monlist database. That is a lot of data, so a relatively small query—for example, the one above is only 48 bytes—can generate a large response, usually in the realm of megabytes. That is the amplification part of the attack. The reflection part is possible because NTP operates over UDP, and a UDP query can easily be forged. In the case of CVE-2013-5211, the attacker identifies a target; finds an NTP server with a large, publicly queryable monlist; and crafts queries that appear to come from the target host. Hence, a low-impact forged query generates a large amount of traffic to the target host, potentially taking it offline.

This is exactly what happened in December of 2013. There was a significant spike in NTP traffic as attackers began taking advantage of this weakness in NTP.

Note   Reading all these vulnerabilities, many security administrators will wonder which version of the NTP daemon is running in the organization, or, more accurately, which versions. This concern will be further heightened if no one can determine when the last time these different daemons were updated. Fortunately, using ntpq, it is relatively easy to find out which version of NTP is running on most Linux or UNIX-type servers. The command to run is: **ntpq -c "rv 0 version"** and the output should look similar to this: **version="ntpd 4.2.6p5@1.2349-o Thu Feb 11 18:30:40 UTC 2016 (1)"**

CVE-2013-5472 concerned a vulnerability in the Cisco IOS versions 12.0 through 12.4 and 15.0 through 15.1. This vulnerability also impacted IOS XE versions 2.1 through 3.3. In this vulnerability, the NTP daemon on the Cisco hardware did not properly respond to NTP requests sent in an encapsulated Multicast Source Discovery Protocol (MSDP) Source-Active (SA) packet from a trusted peer. Vulnerable systems would respond to the packet by reloading. A sustained attack would result in the DoS of the vulnerable router. While this was a critical vulnerability, the attack was unlikely to occur and there are no known public instances of it being exploited. Cisco released a patch quickly.

CVE-2014-9293-CVE-2014-9298 dealt with a number of vulnerabilities that were reported by Neel Mehta and Stephen Roettger, both part of Google's security team and Dieter Sibold, PhD of the Physikalisch-Technische Bundesantalt (the authoritative source of time in Germany). These vulnerabilities were patched as of version 4.2.8p1. Several of these vulnerabilities included flaws in the encryption of the NTP daemon, such as generating a weak default key if the authentication key variable was not set in the ntp.conf file, not validating the vallen packet value in the ntp_crypto.c library, and a buffer overflow in the crypto_recv() function.

CVE-2015-1798 impacted all NTPv4 releases from 4.2.5p99 to 4.2.8p1. This was a vulnerability in the symmetric key authentication. NTP clients and peers that accepted symmetric key authentication would confirm that a valid message authentication code (MAC) was present in the authentication packet, but not if a MAC was present. In other words, if an attacker were to send a client or peer a packet with a blank MAC field, the NTP daemon would treat it the same as a successful authentication. This would allow an attacker to potentially conduct a man-in-the-middle (MITM) attack against a network using symmetric encryption for NTP.

CVE-2015-7871 allowed crypto-NAK packets to force the NTP daemon to accept a time update from temporary peers. First discovered by Matthew Van Gundy at Cisco, this vulnerability affected NTP daemon versions 4.2.5p186 through 4.2.8p3. It also impacted version 4.3.0 through 4.3.76. The cleverly titled "NAK to the Future[1]" allowed an attacker that was not part of an NTP server's peer network to force the victim to sync with an NTP server of the attacker's choosing. Again, this would allow an attacker to throw off an NTP server or client's clock and potentially disrupt network activity.

CVE-2015-7974 was also discovered by a researcher at Cisco, Matt Street, and it involved versions of the NTP daemon prior to 4.2.8p6 and 4.3.90 not verifying the peer associations of symmetric keys. One way that NTP servers can authenticate with each other is to use symmetric keys. In a symmetric authentication setup, if a server has multiple peers, each peer will have their own key. In vulnerable versions, an attacker is able to use a "skeleton key" to authenticate—the server checks to make sure that the key works, but doesn't check to make sure it is the key assigned to that specific peer.

CVE-2016-4956 was a new vulnerability introduced by the fixes to CVE-2016-1548. Versions of the NTP daemon prior to 4.2.8p8 were vulnerable to a DoS attack from a forged broadcast packet.

CVE-2016-4957 was a new vulnerability introduced by the fixes to CVE-2016-1547. This bug impacted versions of the NTP daemon prior to 4.2.8p8 and allowed an attacker to remotely initiate a DoS attack against an NTP server using forged crypto-NAK packets.

CVE-2016-9312 was a high-level vulnerability affecting the Windows version of the NTP daemon, reported in November of 2016. The vulnerability affected all version of the Windows NTP daemon prior to 4.2.8p9 and it allowed an attacker to send a malicious packet that was "too big" to the NTP server. The crafted packet would cause the Windows NTP daemon to shut down.

This list was a quick summary of some of the medium- and high-level vulnerabilities NTP has experienced over many years. It is not an exhaustive list, but it does provide an overview of some of the problems NTP has experienced.

---

[1] The bug was reported in 2015, which was also the 30-year anniversary of the movie *Back to the Future*.

Why Is NTP So Insecure?

With a long list of vulnerabilities in the NTP daemon across multiple platforms, it seems like NTP must be one of the most insecure programs/protocols on the Internet. The truth is that NTP, when implemented properly, is not all that insecure.

Although there certainly have been a number of serious flaws that have plagued NTP over the years, it is important to remember that NTP has a 30-plus-year history of continuous operation. While that does not diminish the seriousness of flaws in NTP, it does give it some context.

Compare the security track record of NTP with an application such as WordPress. Between the base program and its plugins, WordPress has had more than 975 reported vulnerabilities since its inception, as opposed to the roughly 35 or so vulnerabilities reported about the various implementations of NTP during the same time period.

For a more direct comparison, over its lifetime, the Berkeley Internet Name Domain (BIND) DNS server, developed by the Internet Systems Consortium (ISC), has had 68 reported vulnerabilities. Like the Network Time Foundation, ISC has been very responsive, fixing reported vulnerabilities and introducing new security capabilities into the product, making it even more secure.

NTP has developed a reputation for being insecure because when a vulnerability is discovered it impacts so much of the Internet. When a new WordPress vulnerability is reported, most organizations don't care because they are not running instances of WordPress. On the other hand, every organization connected to the Internet is running some variant of NTP. Because of this, NTP vulnerabilities carry an outsized importance and, rightfully, receive outsized attention in the press.

As more vulnerabilities are reported over time, or as those vulnerabilities are used to launch repeated large-scale DDoS attacks, the reports remain present in the minds of network and security administrators. When a new one is reported, it becomes a case of "there goes NTP again—when are they going to fix all of these problems?"

On the other side of the problem is the fact that a lot of organizations have not implemented many of the security capabilities that the Network Time Foundation has added over the years. There are a number of security features built into the NTP daemon that can be used to prevent the NTP server from being used in DDoS attacks. There are more that can be enabled to thwart some zero day vulnerabilities. There are even network configuration options that help keep NTP servers protected from spying eyes. Yet, too many organizations either don't implement them or don't even know they exist.

Credit needs to go to many of the Linux vendors who have started implementing some of these security features by default. The default *ntp.conf* file for Ubuntu, Debian, Red Hat Enterprise Linux, CentOS, and others includes a number of security enhancements such as not allowing queries, peering, or modifications from remote hosts, as shown in Listing 2-2.

Listing 2-2. *Entries in ntp.conf restricting remote access*

```
# By default, exchange time with everybody, but don't allow configuration.
restrict -4 default kod notrap nomodify nopeer noquery
restrict -6 default kod notrap nomodify nopeer noquery
```

But there are vendors who have not taken the same steps to improve the default security of their NTP installations. In those cases, it is incumbent on organizations to understand what security options are available and implement those security options in a timely fashion.

Finally, NTP was originally developed in a different time. While there were certainly malicious actors and worms in 1985, they were not as prevalent. In the original RFC 958, security is not mentioned at all. The RFC for NTP version 4 talks about security 15 different times. There is much more emphasis on security and secure configuration of an NTP installation.

On top of changes to the way the Network Time Foundation thinks about security, they have also gotten more responsive to security reports. In addition to putting out patches in a more timely fashion, they also work closely with the security research community as it uncovers new bugs and vulnerabilities.

Of course, none of this effort on the part of the Network Time Foundation means anything if their recommendations and not heeded. Too often, the version of the NTP that is shipped with a server is never upgraded or changed, even when recommendations from the Network Time Foundation change.

This is really the biggest problem with protocols such at NTP.

The Problem with "Set It and Forget It" Protocols

The problem with NTP is that it falls into a small subset of protocols that are really "set it and forget it." In other words, after the initial configuration, there is really nothing else that network administrator has to do to keep it running. Other protocols on this list include DNS, HTTP/HTTPS, SSH and RDP.

These protocols tend to be forgotten when it comes to security planning because they just work and don't require any updating on the part of the security teams. There may be planning around the programs that operate on top of these protocols, such as web browsers or the websites that operate over HTTP/HTTPS, but the protocols themselves go unnoticed.

That is, until there is a well-publicized vulnerability or, even worse, a well-publicized attack directed at the protocol. At that point, organizations often scramble to understand whether or not they are impacted. It is one thing to secure a web server against cross-site scripting attacks, but does anyone in the organization remember how the HTTP server itself was initially configured? If there is a new DDoS attack that takes advantage of a flaw in NTP, does anyone know how many devices in the network use NTP and how each of those devices is configured?

The answer to these question is generally no, but it doesn't need to be. Just as it is important to understand all of the programs that are installed on desktops and servers throughout the network, understanding what protocols are enabled and how they are configured is a critical component of a successful security program.

It starts with treating these protocols just like an operating system baseline. Most organizations have a "gold image" for servers and workstations, or more accurately, multiple "gold images" depending on the function of the device. These "gold images" have all the programs necessary for the system to function properly in its role, but they also have all of the necessary security patches that the image must maintain in order to comply with the security team.

The same should be done with "set it and forget it" protocols. Security teams should be working with system and networking teams in an organization to create requirements for implementing these protocols across all platforms. For example, for NTP there could be a requirement that any implementation of NTP should use NTP version 4. There could also be a requirement that all NTP-enabled hosts must not allow queries from hosts outside the network. For organizations that have installed their own NTP server, it should be a requirement for all internal hosts to use the internal NTP server. Finally, there should be a requirement that all systems must have a certain version of the NTP daemon installed. This version will change from platform to platform, so it should be clearly documented. It should also be documented how quickly the organization will test and move from one version to the next whenever a new version is released.

Whatever the security requirements for enabling these protocols, the security team should document them clearly. They should also document any use cases that can't meet the outlined security requirements. Those systems that can't meet the requirements should be closely monitored for potential attacks.

Of course, best practices in security change all the time. The last phase of this is to regularly review and update the best security practices for these protocols. As new attack vectors are discovered in the wild, developers will make recommendations for configuration updates and, of course, release new versions. This requires not only updating the configuration for newly deployed systems, but having a plan in place to go back and update existing systems.

None of this is easy, especially in an environment where network, system and security teams are often overworked. Unfortunately, not tracking with current best practices can result in a costly breach of the organization. So, while it does not need to be a full-time job, there should be someone in the organization who is responsible for looking after one or more of the protocols in the network and understanding what the current best practices are. That person should provide regular reporting to the rest of the teams and should be making recommendations for changes as appropriate.

Analysis of NTP Traffic

Before diving into how NTP is exploited, it's important to understand what NTP traffic looks like. Chapter 1 presented an overview of an NTP packet in diagram form, but it is also good to see it in action.

Note The packets used in this section originate from an NTP server maintained by the author, ntp.cryptodns.com, which is part of the pool.ntp.org pool of NTP servers. All third-party IP addresses have been obscured for security purposes.

The first packet is from a machine making an NTP request to ntp.cryptodns.com (line breaks are inserted for readability) as shown in Listing 2-3.

Listing 2-3. A client making a request to a server

```
01:00:31.363495 IP (tos 0x0, ttl 46, id 0, offset 0, flags [DF], proto UDP
(17), length 76)
    192.168.1.30.44404 > ntp.cryptodns.com.ntp: [udp sum ok] NTPv3, length 48
        Client, Leap indicator:  (0), Stratum 0 (unspecified), poll 0 (1s),
        precision 0
        Root Delay: 0.000000, Root dispersion: 0.000000, Reference-ID:
        (unspec)
          Reference Timestamp:   0.000000000
          Originator Timestamp:  0.000000000
          Receive Timestamp:     0.000000000
          Transmit Timestamp:     3678998430.149000003 (2016/08/01 01:00:30)
            Originator - Receive Timestamp:   0.000000000
            Originator - Transmit Timestamp: 3678998430.149000003
(2016/08/01 01:00:30)
```

The first two lines in the example above are part of the UDP header, indicating the source host, destination host, source port, destination port (NTP), length of the pack, and version of NTP. In this case, the host is sending an NTPv3 request, which means the NTP server will respond with an NTPv3 response.

The third line starts with the actual NTP packet. The first field indicates the mode, which in this case is "client," of the requesting host, and that it is not a Leap Second packet (which would not originate from a client). The client has a stratum of 0, which is the stratum associated with clients that have never connected to a remote NTP server (true stratum 0 servers are reference clocks to which stratum 1 servers have a direct connection). The poll exponent is set to 0, which most likely means it is the first time that this client has contacted this server—however, it could also indicate a reset. The precision field indicates the precision of the system clock expressed in log base 2 (usually written as log2) seconds. Again, a value of 0 indicates that this is the first communication between the client and server, or that there has been a reset.

Because this is the first time the source host has queried this clock, the root delay and root dispersion are set to 0, while the reference-ID, the name of the reference time source, is unspecified—expected behavior from a client.

Listing 2-4 shows the response from the server. Note that the response is NTPv3 compliant, since the original request was an NTPv3 request. The mode in this case is set to server, while the stratum is set to 2, which most NTP servers in the NTP Pool Project are. The poll is set to 3 log2 or 8 seconds, which is the maximum interval between messages on this server. The precision of the clock on the responding server is set to -20 log2, or less than a microsecond (1/1000000 of a second).

The root delay is the round-trip delay to the reference clock, and the root dispersion is the difference in time between the server and the correct time (the time provided by the stratum 1 server). Finally, the reference-ID, in this case darkcity.cerias.purdue.edu, is the stratum 1 server from which the stratum 2 server gets its time.

Listing 2-4. Response from the server to the client

```
01:00:31.363586 IP (tos 0xc0, ttl 64, id 17769, offset 0, flags [DF], proto
UDP (17), length 76)
  ntp.cryptodns.com.ntp > 192.168.1.30.44404: [udp sum ok] NTPv3, length 48
        Server, Leap indicator:  (0), Stratum 2 (secondary reference), poll
        3 (8s), precision -20
        Root Delay: 0.032821, Root dispersion: 0.041763, Reference-ID:
        darkcity.cerias.purdue.edu
          Reference Timestamp:  3678997837.299738913 (2016/08/01 00:50:37)
          Originator Timestamp: 3678998430.149000003 (2016/08/01 01:00:30)
          Receive Timestamp:    3678998431.363495409 (2016/08/01 01:00:31)
          Transmit Timestamp:   3678998431.363574236 (2016/08/01 01:00:31)
            Originator - Receive Timestamp:  +1.214495420
            Originator - Transmit Timestamp: +1.214574232
```

Listing 2-5 is a slightly different example. This query is an NTPv4 query, though all the same fields are present as in the previous example. The first pair of packets shows the first time these two hosts are communicating. The Leap Indicator field shows an unsynchronized clock, and the client has set itself at stratum 0 operating in client mode.

Listing 2-5. *Client connecting to an NTP server*

```
21:55:38.217609 IP (tos 0xc0, ttl 64, id 40800, offset 0, flags [DF], proto
UDP (17), length 76)
    192.168.1.77.ntp > ntp.cryptodns.com.ntp: [udp sum ok] NTPv4, length 48
        Client, Leap indicator: clock unsynchronized (192), Stratum 0
(unspecified), poll 6 (64s), precision -23
        Root Delay: 0.000000, Root dispersion: 0.000991, Reference-ID:
(unspec)
            Reference Timestamp:   0.000000000
            Originator Timestamp: 3679091672.225474119 (2016/08/01 21:54:32)
            Receive Timestamp:    3679091672.233604848 (2016/08/01 21:54:32)
            Transmit Timestamp:   3679091738.217555865 (2016/08/01 21:55:38)
              Originator - Receive Timestamp:  +0.008130721
              Originator - Transmit Timestamp: +65.992081761
21:55:38.228064 IP (tos 0x0, ttl 53, id 19741, offset 0, flags [DF], proto
UDP (17), length 76)
    ntp.cryptodns.com.ntp > 192.168.1.77.ntp: [udp sum ok] NTPv4, length 48
        Server, Leap indicator:  (0), Stratum 2 (secondary reference), poll
        6 (64s), precision -20
        Root Delay: 0.033676, Root dispersion: 0.041046, Reference-ID:
        darkcity.cerias.purdue.edu
          Reference Timestamp:   3679091211.681040108 (2016/08/01 21:46:51)
          Originator Timestamp: 3679091738.217555865 (2016/08/01 21:55:38)
          Receive Timestamp:    3679091738.225709989 (2016/08/01 21:55:38)
          Transmit Timestamp:   3679091738.225783973 (2016/08/01 21:55:38)
            Originator - Receive Timestamp:  +0.008154135
            Originator - Transmit Timestamp: +0.008228117
```

However, in the second set of queries, after the servers have been talking for several hours, the stratum is set to 3. The client still identifies itself as such, but it can now also operate as a stratum 3 server, and it has set its reference clock as ntp.cryptodns.com, the server clock.

All of this happened automatically; there were no changes that needed to be made to the configuration of the client server. The NTP daemon did all of the work and made the changes—see Listing 2-6.

Listing 2-6. *NTP server response to the client*

```
00:51:14.326353 IP (tos 0xc0, ttl 64, id 64539, offset 0, flags [DF], proto
UDP (17), length 76)
    192.168.1.77.ntp > ntp.cryptodns.com.com.ntp: [udp sum ok] NTPv4, length 48
        Client, Leap indicator:  (0), Stratum 3 (secondary reference), poll
        6 (64s), precision -23
        Root Delay: 0.040283, Root dispersion: 1.013671, Reference-ID: ntp.
        cryptodns.com
            Reference Timestamp:   3679102207.333402454 (2016/08/02 00:50:07)
            Originator Timestamp: 3679102207.316343069 (2016/08/02 00:50:07)
            Receive Timestamp:     3679102207.333402454 (2016/08/02 00:50:07)
            Transmit Timestamp:    3679102274.326300173 (2016/08/02 00:51:14)
              Originator - Receive Timestamp:   +0.017059391
              Originator - Transmit Timestamp: +67.009957099
00:51:14.334436 IP (tos 0x0, ttl 53, id 20022, offset 0, flags [DF], proto
UDP (17), length 76)
    ntp.cryptodns.com.ntp > 192.168.1.77.ntp: [udp sum ok] NTPv4, length 48
        Server, Leap indicator:  (0), Stratum 2 (secondary reference), poll
        6 (64s), precision -20
        Root Delay: 0.033264, Root dispersion: 0.041809, Reference-ID:
        darkcity.cerias.purdue.edu
            Reference Timestamp:   3679101761.680720388 (2016/08/02 00:42:41)
            Originator Timestamp: 3679102274.326300173 (2016/08/02 00:51:14)
            Receive Timestamp:     3679102274.321736901 (2016/08/02 00:51:14)
            Transmit Timestamp:    3679102274.321832090 (2016/08/02 00:51:14)
              Originator - Receive Timestamp:   -0.004563249
              Originator - Transmit Timestamp: -0.004468078
```

The only change that cannot be automatically made in the NTP configuration is the jump from a stratum 2 to a stratum 1 server. As outlined previously, stratum 1 servers must be attached to a reference clock. No matter how accurate a stratum 2 server is (as seen above, with today's computing power and network speeds, a stratum 2 server can maintain sub-microsecond accuracy), it cannot jump up to stratum 1.

Conclusions

While NTP has a long list of well-published security vulnerabilities, NTP is not any more insecure than dozens of other widely deployed applications. In fact, compared to some, NTP's track record when it comes to fixing security holes is admirable.

In reality, NTP's biggest problem is one of entropy. Because the NTP daemon works so well and is able to adapt to changing network environment on the fly, it gets very little attention from network and security teams. This means that updates and security configuration recommendations are not always heeded, or even seen.

In order to more effectively secure an NTP installation, it is incumbent on the security team to keep up to date on the latest developments in NTP security. Watching for security alerts on the NTP web site, subscribing to mailing lists, or even using a third party that tracks vulnerabilities are all ways that a security team can manage new NTP vulnerabilities and make changes as NTP security changes.

Vulnerabilities in NTP

Having reviewed some of the issues in NTP security, the next step is to take a closer look at some of the vulnerabilities. The goal of this chapter is not to cover specific vulnerabilities, but instead look at how vulnerabilities in NTP can be exploited and the potential damage those exploits can cause to an organization.

This chapter will review examples of vulnerabilities that have occurred in four areas of attack: the daemon, the protocol, the encryption process, and authentication. The last two, encryption and authentication, are rarely deployed, even though they should be. Making use of authentication and encryption makes it more difficult for attackers to take advantage of the last security risk: the use of NTP packets in the Distributed Denial of Service (DDoS) attack.

Vulnerabilities in the Daemon

Unpatched vulnerabilities in the NTP daemon, especially those that are remotely executable, are of particular concern to an organization because they potentially allow an attacker access to the network. A remotely executable vulnerability can do a lot of damage depending on the user that is running the NTP daemon:

```
ntp Ss Aug02 336:41 /usr/sbin/ntpd -p /var/run/ntpd.pid -g -u 105:112
```

© Allan Liska 2016
A. Liska, *NTP Security*, DOI 10.1007/978-1-4842-2412-0_3

Note that in this example the NTP daemon is running as the user "ntp," an unprivileged user with limited access to the system. However, that is not always the case—some systems run the NTP daemon as root. So, if an attacker gains access by exploiting an NTP vulnerability, she has unlimited access to the system.

■ **Note** The focus of this section will be on the NTP reference implementation available at www. ntp.org. This is the most widely deployed version of the NTP daemon and is the basis for most NTP implementations in use today.

Again, it should be noted that the developers at the Network Time Project take security very seriously, and there have been relatively few recent vulnerabilities that have allowed remote execution on the victim server. The bigger problem is that system administrators don't patch the NTP daemon frequently. Beyond that, even system administrators who do regularly update their systems are at the mercy of software vendors who don't always provide packages for the latest version of the NTP daemon.

This leaves system administrators and security teams with a quandary: should they use the daemon available from the Network Time Project and be forced to check back regularly for updates? Or should they use the package provided by their distribution vendor and take advantage of automated updates, even if some of those updates are slow coming? Neither option is ideal.

To understand vulnerabilities against the NTP daemon, it is worth looking at CVE-2014-9295. Remember, CVE-2014-9295 is a buffer overflow vulnerability in all versions of the NTP daemon prior to 4.2.8.

There were actually three different buffer overflows in different functions of the code: crypto_recv(), ctl_putdata(), and configure(). Each of these buffer overflow conditions would allow an attacker to send arbitrary code that would be executed at the privilege level of the user running the NTP daemon. If that user doesn't have any privileges, as in the previous example, the damage to the system could be minimal. However, if that user is running as root, the damage to the organization could be severe.

Let's take a step back for a second and define what a buffer overflow is. A buffer overflow occurs when input sent to a buffer in a program exceeds the boundary for that particular buffer, or when the program tries to place data in memory outside of the buffer. What does this mean in practical terms? A program accepts inputs at different points in the execution process, but there is a limit to how much data can be sent at any one time. When the amount of data sent exceeds the amount that can be handled by a particular buffer, the program can reject it, drop it, or, if there are no protections in place, allow the data to continue coming. That data will overflow the buffer and start filling up the memory of the system. At its least insidious, a buffer overflow can cause a program to crash, knocking the service offline. However, sometimes the program will crash while still feeding that data into memory. In these cases, the attacker can embed a lightweight executable, called a loader, into the data stream along with the command to execute. When the targeted program crashes, the loader will be executed and call back to the attacker's command and control infrastructure, potentially giving the attacker access to the vulnerable system.

In this case, there were three functions in the NTP daemon that were potentially impacted by a buffer overflow vulnerability. One of these, configure(), looked to be relatively easy to exploit (it should be noted that, as of this writing, there is no known exploit for vulnerability).

This vulnerability was particularly dangerous because it applied to any NTP host running in server mode and it could be exploited remotely. An attacker with a well-formed packet from a spoofed IP address could exploit NTP and use that exploitation to gain access to the server.

What does a buffer overflow vulnerability look like? Generally, it is simply the absence of error handling code for a buffer. In this case, there was no boundary checking in place. To understand, first see the code as it was prior to the patch[1] in Listing 3-1.

Listing 3-1. NPT daemon remote configuration buffer code with an unpatched buffer overflow

```
/* Initialize the remote config buffer */
data_count = reqend - reqpt;
memcpy(remote_config.buffer, reqpt, data_count);
if (data_count > 0
    && '\n' != remote_config.buffer[data_count - 1])
```

And the code after the vulnerability was patched, looks like Listing 3-2:

Listing 3-2. NTP daemon remote configuration buffer with patches in place

```
/* Initialize the remote config buffer */
data_count = reqend - reqpt;

if (data_count > sizeof(remote_config.buffer) - 2) {
      snprintf(remote_config.err_msg,
             sizeof(remote_config.err_msg),
             "runtime configuration failed: request too long");
      ctl_putdata(remote_config.err_msg,
             strlen(remote_config.err_msg), 0);
```

---

[1]Both code samples retrieved from the NTP Project Bug Page at http://bugs.ntp.org/ attachment.cgi?id=1159&action=diff, accessed August 14, 2016.

```
        ctl_flushpkt(0);
        msyslog(LOG_NOTICE,
                "runtime config from %s rejected: request too long",
                stoa(&rbufp->recv_srcadr));
        return;
}
memcpy(remote_config.buffer, reqpt, data_count);
if (data_count > 0
    && '\n' != remote_config.buffer[data_count - 1])
```

Note that the new code adds a check to ensure that the amount of data being sent doesn't exceed the limits set for the buffer. If more data is sent, the data is dropped and an event is logged to the Syslog facility.

How does an attacker exploit this vulnerability? To demonstrate this, take a look at CVE-2001-0414, an earlier buffer overflow vulnerability in the NTP daemon. This is a very out-of-date vulnerability that most NTP servers are patched against, but there is an exploit module in the Metasploit exploit kit. This makes it easy to see how the exploit works.

CVE-2001-0414 is a buffer overflow in the NTP daemon that potentially allows an attacker to execute arbitrary code by issuing an invalid readvar command that contains too much data. Take a look at the code snippet from the Metasploit module[2] in Listing 3-3.

Listing 3-3. *Metasploit code snippet*

```
hunter  = generate_egghunter(payload.encoded, payload_badchars, { :checksum
=> true })
egg     = hunter[1]

connect_udp
pkt1 = "\x16\x02\x00\x01\x00\x00\x00\x00\x00\x00\x016stratum="
pkt2 = "\x16\x02\x00\x02\x00\x00\x00\x00\x00\x00\x00\x00"

sploit =  pkt1 + make_nops(512 - pkt1.length)
sploit[(220 + pkt1.length), 4] = [target['Ret']].pack('V')
sploit[(224 + pkt1.length), hunter[0].length] = hunter[0]
```

The setup is pretty simple; the module prepares a loader and then prepares two specially crafted NTP packets (pkt1 and pkt2). The attacker simply has to point Metasploit at the target server. The module first sends the forged pkt1 over, and then sends pkt2 to conduct the actual overflow, shown in Listing 3-4.

---

[2]Metasploit code retrieved from the Metasploit GitHub page at https://github.com/rapid7/metasploit-framework/blob/master/modules/exploits/multi/ntp/ntp_overflow.rb, accessed August 14, 2016.

Listing 3-4. Sending the UDP packets to exploit the target NTP server

```
print_status("Sending hunter")
udp_sock.put(sploit)
select(nil,nil,nil,0.5)

print_status("Sending payload")
udp_sock.put(pkt1 + egg)
select(nil,nil,nil,0.5)

print_status("Calling overflow trigger")
udp_sock.put(pkt2)
```

If a buffer overflow is so easy to exploit, why don't developers do more to limit the amount of data that can be sent to a buffer? There are a couple of different answers to this question.

The first is that many application developers are not security experts, so as they are developing programs they may not think about buffer overflows—at least not until the first time one is discovered and exploited. Unfortunately, by the time that happens, it is often too late. In an application of any size, there are thousands of potential buffer overflow points in the program. Remember, any point where data can be input has the potential for a buffer overflow, even if there is no human interaction.

That creates a special problem for developers of programs like the NTP daemon, which has a long history and contributions from multiple developers over time. Going back through the codebase looking for potential buffer overflows is a monotonous and time-consuming task that has to be done while still making improvements to the code. This means it is unlikely that every buffer overflow in the current code base will be uncovered and patched.

On the other hand, because the NTP daemon is open source, there are developers around the world looking at the code. Many of the reported buffer overflows in the current code base have been discovered and reported by third-party developers and fixed quickly by the current NTP development team. This has resulted in significantly fewer buffer overflow reports over the past few years.

The second reason buffer overflows are hard to protect against is that attackers discover new attack vectors for buffer overflows. A method of buffer overflow that may have been unknown five years ago may suddenly be exploitable. Both attackers and security researchers are always looking for new methods of exploitation, so even code developed with security in mind can be susceptible to new forms of attack.

Fortunately, the developers at the NTP project have been very responsive to reports of new attack vectors and have worked quickly to patch the code and respond to new threats.

Vulnerabilities in the Protocol

Although vulnerabilities in the code of the NTP daemon may present the biggest risk to the organization, vulnerabilities in the NTP protocol are the most common.

Part of the risk inherent in NTP is the use of UDP as its transport protocol. UDP is a connectionless Internet Protocol, meaning there is no requirement for confirmation of a successful connection. Unlike protocols that rely on TCP for transport, which do require confirmation of a connection via a three-way handshake, NTP delivered over UDP requires no confirmation that the connection is coming from the original source. In practice, this means that people can do things like issue the command in Listing 3-5 with UDP.

Listing 3-5. *Sending spoofed packet using the hping command*

```
allan@allan-1015E:~$ sudo hping3 ntp.cryptodns.com -V --udp -p 123
--spoof 8.8.8.8 --data 500 using wlan1, addr: 192.168.1.7, MTU: 1500
HPING ntp.cryptodns.com (wlan1 198.84.61.242): udp mode set, 28
headers + 500 data bytes
```

In this example, using the tool hping3, 500 bytes of random data are being sent to the server ntp.cryptodns.com from the spoofed IP address *8.8.8.8*, which is one of the Google DNS servers. On the receiving server, the incoming traffic looks like the packet capture shown in Listing 3-6.

Listing 3-6. *View of the spoofed traffic from the previous hping command*

```
15:28:31.120250 IP (tos 0x0, ttl 64, id 49704, offset 0, flags [none], proto
UDP (17), length 528)
google-public-dns-a.google.com.2908 > ntp.cryptodns.com.ntp: [udp sum
ok] NTPv4, length 500 unspecified, Leap indicator: +1s (64), Stratum 88
(reserved), poll 88 (16777216s), precision 88
Root Delay: 22616.345092, Root dispersion: 22616.345092, Reference-ID:
ti0203a400-1361.bb.online.no
          Reference Timestamp:  1482184792.345098048 (2083/01/25 23:28:08)
          Originator Timestamp: 1482184792.345098048 (2083/01/25 23:28:08)
          Receive Timestamp:    1482184792.345098048 (2083/01/25 23:28:08)
          Transmit Timestamp:   1482184792.345098048 (2083/01/25 23:28:08)
            Originator - Receive Timestamp:   -0.000000000
            Originator - Transmit Timestamp:  -0.000000000
```

As far as the receiving host can tell, the request came in from the Google DNS server, and that is where it would send the response. This is a major flaw with the UDP transport mechanism, because there is no connection between the two hosts and it is easy to spoof a connection.

Spoofing packets means that UDP-based protocols are uniquely susceptible for use in DDoS attacks, which are discussed later in this chapter. It also means that protocols like NTP are susceptible to forged packets. Those forged packets can be used to disrupt the protocol and even crash NTP. A perfect example of this is with CVE-2009-3563, in which a spoofed NTP packet with the mode 7 flag set would cause an NTP daemon to crash.

This was covered briefly in Chapter 1, but it is worth a quick review. Although there are three protocol modes in NTP version 4 (symmetric, client/server, and broadcast), there are six different association modes that are flagged in NTP packets. Those modes are:

1.   Mode 1 – Symmetric Active

2.   Mode 2 – Symmetric Passive

3.   Mode 3 – Client

4.   Mode 4 – Server

5.   Mode 5 – Broadcast Server

6.   Mode 6 – Broadcast Client

So although there are only three modes, there are six possible flags associated with those modes in NTP version 4. However, in prior versions of NTP, there was a Mode 7, which was a reserved mode. Mode 7 is still recognized by NTP version 4 servers for the purpose of backwards compatibility.

In the case of the CVE-2009-3563, an attacker could send a forged packet that had Mode 7 set and a payload of 0x17 (an invalid hex value) and the NTP server would respond to what it thought was the original sender with an error response. The second server would then respond to the target server with an error response and the cycle would continue until all memory on both servers was used up and the systems would crash.

For an even cleaner attack, the attacker could spoof the packet so it looked like it originated from the target server itself. The server would continue to respond to itself in a loop, eating up a little more memory each time until it finally crashed, essentially issuing a DoS attack against itself.

Ultimately, the vulnerability in this instance was with error handling within the NTP daemon, but it was enabled by the fact that an attacker could easily spoof packets. This allowed an attacker to take advantage of a vulnerability that otherwise might not have been easily exploited.

Flaws in NTP Encryption and Authentication

Version 4 of NTP introduced a number of improvements in the encryption process used by NTP for authentication and integrity checking. This is an important distinction: NTP does not maintain a facility to encrypt NTP traffic itself. Instead, NTP encryption is used only for the authentication process. Therefore, it is almost impossible to separate NTP encryption from the authentication process and vice versa.

Note There are versions of NTP that do support encrypted communication, but the reference build, which is what this book has focused on because it is the most widely deployed, does not. Chapter 6 will discuss a number of NTP daemon variants that support encrypted communication.

Encrypted authentication is important, as it helps to ensure that an incoming message is able to be verified. However, by not encrypting the data packets NTP traffic is subject to monitoring by an attacker sitting between a client and server or between a pool of servers.

So what? Generally, there is no sensitive data contained within an NTP packet, so it doesn't really matter if an attacker can snoop it. Unfortunately, it can make a difference. To this point in the book, there has been little discussion around some of the more advanced attacks that can only be carried out by someone who is able to inspect NTP traffic, primarily because these attacks are rare, and in cases where they can be carried out there are usually other, "low-hanging fruit" type of attacks that make more sense and don't potentially expose other systems controlled by the attackers.

The fact is, there are a number of advanced hacking groups, including nation states, with the type of accesses that would allow them to inspect NTP packets and use that information to carry out a complex attack.

Symmetric Encryption

NTP version 3 supported the use of symmetric key encryption for authentication and verification purposes. NTP version 4 maintains backwards compatibility with this feature. Symmetric-key encryption uses the same key to encrypt and decrypt the data. This requires the key to be stored by both the sender and the receiver in order to encrypt and decrypt the message. Thus, symmetric-key encryption is vulnerable to attack if an attacker has access to either the sender's or the receiver's system.

Setting up the keys is a two-part process. The first step is to identify where the keyfile is in the ntp.conf file:

```
### Authentication section ###
keys /etc/ntp/keys
```

While doing that, it is also important to identify which hosts require keys in order to connect to the client or server:

```
server ntp.cryptodns.com key 5
```

The key number is a unique identifier assigned to each host (or every host can use the same identifier), and it must be a 16-bit number between 1 and 65535.

The keys file, defined in the ntp.conf file, contains statements similar to those in Listing 3-7.

Listing 3-7. Sample keys file

```
#
# PLEASE DO NOT USE THE DEFAULT VALUES HERE.
#
#65535  M  [password]
#1      M  pass
5  M  s3cur3NTP
```

The format of the keys file is simple. Each line contains the key number, the key type, and the password, or key, itself.

In the example above, unique key identifier 5, which is assigned to ntp.cryptodns.com, is assigned the MD5 hashed password s3cur3NTP. This same setup will need to be mirrored on the server side as well, so that the server will know that it needs to authenticate the client with that password.

Obviously, there are a number of security problems with this setup, not the least of which is the fact that storing unencrypted passwords in a file on the client and server makes them an easy target. Not to mention that every time this password is changed, it has to be sent to one or more hosts in a secure manner, causing many potential weak points in the chain that can be exploited by an attacker.

Unfortunately, that is not the only problem. As mentioned briefly in Chapter 2, CVE-2015-1798 and CVE-2015-1799 both identified bugs in symmetric authentication that could allow an attacker to bypass this security measure. In the case of CVE-2015-1798, NTP version 4 between versions 4.2.5p99 and 4.2.8p2 were vulnerable to a flaw in which NTP was checking to make sure that incoming packets had a valid message authentication code (MAC), but not if the incoming messages had the actual MAC.

In other words, a bad guy sniffing traffic between a client and server could forge packets indicating that they had a valid MAC, even if the MAC was not included in the message, and the NTP client or server on the other end would accept those packets as if they had a valid MAC included. This would allow the attacker to bypass authentication systems enabled by the NTP administrators.

CVE-2015-1799 is another example where symmetric authentication should have prevented an attack from happening, but wouldn't have been able to. CVE-2015-1799 was a DoS vulnerability that existed in all versions of NTP prior to 4.2.8p2. The vulnerability itself existed between two symmetrically peered hosts. An attacker could have sent a forged packet to host A, which appeared to have originated from peering host B. The forged packet would contain incorrect NTP state variables. Host A would update with the new variables, and when it sent its next update to host B, it would have different variables. Eventually, the different state variables would cause the two hosts to de-peer and the two hosts would not be able to synchronize with each other.

Symmetric authentication between the two peering hosts should make an attack like this unworkable. However, as it turns out, the updated state information was being passed to the peering host prior to the authentication being processed. So, even if the packet was rejected with a bad MAC, the NTP state information from the forged packet would still be processed.

The fix to this was simple: process NTP state information after the symmetric authentication was successfully processed. As stated above, this fix is implemented in versions 4.2.8p2 and later of NTP.

AutoKey

NTP version 4 introduced a public key encryption security model known as AutoKey. AutoKey is not a true Public Key Infrastructure (PKI) security model. Making use of PKI would put too great a strain on the time synchronization aspect of NTP, so while it would increase the security of the protocol, it would do so at the expense of its primary purpose: synching time.

Instead, AutoKey relies on a combination of public keys and a pseudo-random sequence of hashes. This was explained in more detail in Chapter 1. AutoKey is a lightweight but cryptographically secure method of authentication. Similar to the Domain Name System Security Extensions (DNSSEC) protocol, AutoKey is delivered from the top down. This means that an NTP client can't initiate an AutoKey sequence, but its server can (of course, like DNSSEC, the client has to be configured to accept it).

AutoKey provides a stronger encrypted authentication sequence than symmetric key encryption, but it has still had a few security issues. Note that none of the security issues have involved the encryption itself—only the implementation of the encryption.

Probably the biggest flaw in the AutoKey implementation was reported in the previously discussed CVE-2014-9295. This vulnerability allowed an attacker to exploit a buffer overflow in the crypto_recv function and possibly execute code. The vulnerability was so critical that the developers of NTP recommended users disable AutoKey until the patch could be delivered. The good/bad news is that, given the complexity of setting up AutoKey and the relatively poor documentation, not many users appear to be taking advantage of AutoKey, so it does not seem that too many people were affected.

To understand how this buffer overflow worked, take a look at the patched code[3] in Listing 3-8.

Listing 3-8. Patched AutoKey buffer overflow code

```
--- a/ntpd/ntp_crypto.c
+++ b/ntpd/ntp_crypto.c
@@ -792,15 +792,24 @@ crypto_recv(
                         * errors.
                         */
                        if (vallen == (u_int)EVP_PKEY_size(host_pkey)) {
+                               u_int32 *cookiebuf = malloc(
+                                   RSA_size(host_pkey->pkey.rsa));
+                               if (!cookiebuf) {
+                                       rval = XEVNT_CKY;
+                                       break;
+                               }
+
                               if (RSA_private_decrypt(vallen,
                                   (u_char *)ep->pkt,
-                                  (u_char *)&temp32,
+                                  (u_char *)cookiebuf,
                                   host_pkey->pkey.rsa,
-                                  RSA_PKCS1_OAEP_PADDING) <= 0) {
+                                  RSA_PKCS1_OAEP_PADDING) != 4) {
                                       rval = XEVNT_CKY;
+                                      free(cookiebuf);
                                       break;
                               } else {
-                                      cookie = ntohl(temp32);
+                                      cookie = ntohl(*cookiebuf);
+                                      free(cookiebuf);
                               }
                        } else {
                               rval = XEVNT_CKY;
```

---

[3]Code sample retrieved from the NTP Project Bug Page at: http://bugs.ntp.org/show_bug.cgi?id=2667, accessed August 16, 2016

Note that the patch delivered by Stephen Röttger fixes the buffer for the received RSA key. The original buffer was limited to four bytes when the buffer should have been dynamically allocated to allow for whatever size the incoming RSA key was.

Although that may have been the most serious, it is not the only bug associated with AutoKey. In May of 2016, Miroslav Lichvar of Red Hat reported a vulnerability that wound up being CVE-2016-4955, which allowed an attacker sitting in a network to force a dissociation between two peers with AutoKey enabled. This bug was resolved in June 2016.

This bug impacts all version of NTP before 4.2.8p8. This bug only impacted NTP hosts that had a peering relationship secured with AutoKey. An attacker could send a packet with spoofed crypt-NAKs or a bad MAC, which would eventually force the target host to call the peer_clear() function and disconnect from all associated peers, causing time between those peers to eventually fall out of synchronization.

Unlike the previous example, this is not a coding error; this is the way AutoKey is designed to work. The problem is that the AutoKey implementation did not take into account that these types of attack might happen. In this case, the problem was fixed by adjusting the order of operations. Prior to calling the peer_clear() function, NTP now checks to make sure the packets aren't spoofed by checking that the origin timestamp matches the transmit timestamp.

CVE-2014-9750 is another vulnerability involving AutoKey that was potentially so dangerous that the NTP developers recommended disabling AutoKey until the patch could be released. This vulnerability impacted versions of NTP prior to 4.2.8p1 and could possibly have resulted in the NTP daemon crashing or an information leak.

The vulnerability existed in the vallen packets within the NTP cryptographic libraries. There was no proper validation of the data, which could result in an incorrect processing of the packets, as the data would not necessarily be in the proper format as it is passed through the cryptographic libraries.

NTP Use in DDoS Attacks

The most well-publicized vulnerability in NTP is not necessarily a vulnerability. The fact that NTP is susceptible to DDoS attacks is due in large part to the fact that NTP runs over UDP. UDP is a connectionless protocol that can be easily forged, making it easy to trick one or more hosts on the Internet to send massive amounts of traffic to a target host with very little bandwidth expenditure on the part of the attacker.

The difference between a DoS, like the attacks described to this point in the chapter, and a DDoS attack is that the purpose of a DoS attack is to make a service or host unavailable remotely from a single attack point. A DDoS attack uses multiple remote hosts, spread across the Internet, and one or more intermediary hosts to launch a large, bandwidth-consuming attack on a target host or network.

The monlist query attack, documented in Chapter 2, is one example of this, but really any query that produces results which are significantly larger than the original query will do. This is known as a DDoS amplification attack.

These types of DDoS amplification attacks are not limited to NTP. DNS and the Simple Service Discovery Protocol (SSDP) are among the other UDP-based protocols that are often used to attack target hosts. Any service that relies on UDP and offers the ability for small queries to return large amounts of data can be used to launch a DDoS attack.

In fact, along with monlist, the ntpdc commands support a number of commands that generate more traffic than the incoming query, such as:

1. Peers

2. Iostats

3. Sysinfo

None of these commands will generate as much traffic as the monlist command, but they can still do a lot of damage if remote hosts are allowed to run the commands and redirect the traffic.

The same problem pops up with the ntpq command. There are a number of queries ntpq can make that will output more traffic than generated by the original request—often substantially more. For example, a command like ntpq −c lpeers, shown in Listing 3-9.

Listing 3-9. Output of the lpeers command

```
root@server:~# ntpq -c lpeers
     remote           refid      st t when poll reach   delay  offset jitter
==============================================================================
 206.246.118.250 .INIT.          16 u    - 1024    0   0.000  0.000   0.000
  clock.via.net  199.102.46.73    2 u 167m 1024    0  80.112 -5.708   0.000
+darkcity.cerias .GPS.            1 u  995 1024  377 105.427 -42.965 53.991
*clock.fmt.he.ne .CDMA.           1 u  305 1024   77  69.033  -7.751  4.495
```

Another example would be the command ntpq −c readlist, demonstrated in Listing 3-10

Listing 3-10. Output of the readlist command

```
root@server:~# ntpq -c readlist
associd=0 status=0615 leap_none, sync_ntp, 1 event, clock_sync,
version="ntpd 4.2.6p5@1.2349-o Thu Feb 11 18:30:40 UTC 2016 (1)",
processor="x86_64", system="Linux/3.13.0-93-generic", leap=00, stratum=2,
precision=-22, rootdelay=69.033, rootdisp=108.479, refid=216.218.192.202,
reftime=db9713b4.47962e8d  Thu, Aug 11 2016  5:14:44.279,
clock=db97191d.73a7ebb8  Thu, Aug 11 2016  5:37:49.451, peer=14122,
tc=10, mintc=3, offset=-17.827, frequency=-1.365, sys_jitter=18.267,
clk_jitter=9.533, clk_wander=1.069
```

Not only is this command a potential vector for a DDoS attack, but it also reveals a great deal of data about the intermediary system. So, if the server allows remote queries, there is a twofold danger of a data leak and the server acting as a redirect for a DDoS attack.

■ **Note**   Often, system administrators will configure NTP so that it does not allow these types of queries from remote hosts, but will allow the queries to be made from the local host. That is perfectly acceptable—they are often useful queries for troubleshooting purposes. However, a big mistake many administrators make is to allow queries from 127.0.0.1 (the loopback address).

On many systems, the loopback address can be spoofed, so allowing queries from 127.0.0.1 gives attackers an obvious source IP address to use in the spoofing part of their amplification attack. Allow configuration from the host address, but not the loopback address.

Primarily because of the monlist query vulnerability, DDoS attacks saw a resurgence in 2014 and have continued to rise. Many of the largest networks have taken steps to protect potential victims from being targeted by NTP DDoS attacks, or being used as a redirector. But that still leaves millions of vulnerable hosts, primarily home routers that are rarely patched, that can be used to launch these attacks.

Make no mistake: these attacks can be massive, and they can overwhelm even the most robust network. In 2014, the largest DDoS attack ever launched (to that point) was reported by CloudFlare to be more than 400 gigabits per second and was based on the NTP monlist reflection attack[4].

There are also a number of tools that make it easy to launch these attacks with very little effort on the part of the attacker. These so-called NTP-AMP (short for NTP amplification) toolkits come in a range of formats, from nicely developed tools with a slick GUI interface, such as Lizard Stresser [sic], to simpler, Python-based tools, such as ntpdos.

---

[4]Schwartz, Mathew. "DDoS Attack Hits 400 Gbit/s, Breaks Record." *Dark Reading*, UBM, Nov. 2, 2014. Accessed Aug. 31, 2016.

Most of the Python NTP-AMP toolkits rely on the Scapy Python library to create the forged packets. According to its developer, "Scapy is a powerful packet manipulation program"—in other words, it can be used to forge packets and launch attacks.

It should be noted that Scapy is a great tool for system administrators. It helps administrators troubleshoot network problems, recreate traffic flow in the network, decode a number of common protocols, and more. So, even though in this use case it is used to launch an attack, it is actually a very good tool for day-to-day network troubleshooting.

However, like most powerful administrative tools, it can also be used for attacking hosts. Using the ntpdos code in Listing 3-11, which is typical of NTP-AMP toolkits, from GitHub[5] the attack is fairly routine.

Listing 3-11. Running the ntpdos toolkit

```
root@server:/tmp# python ntpdos.py
NTP Amplification DOS Attack
By DaRkReD
Usage ntpdos.py <target ip> <ntpserver list> <number of threads>
ex: ex: ntpdos.py 1.2.3.4 file.txt 10
NTP serverlist file should contain one IP per line
MAKE SURE YOUR THREAD COUNT IS LESS THAN OR EQUAL TO YOUR NUMBER OF SERVERS
```

The Python code only requires a user to enter a target host and provide a file with a list of redirect servers, plus a thread count—the script takes care of everything else.

Creating each spoofed packet is relatively simple in the code, and relies on the capabilities built into Scapy, shown in Listing 3-12 (line break in line 4 inserted for readability)

Listing 3-12. Output of the Scapy command

```
ntpserver = ntplist[currentserver] #Get new server
currentserver = currentserver + 1 #Increment for next
packet =IP(dst=ntpserver,src=target)/UDP(sport=random.randint(2000,65535),
        dport=12        3)/Raw(load=data) #BUILD IT
send(packet,loop=1) #SEND IT
```

The Scapy calls build the forged packet, but it still requires the monlist request to be inserted:

```
#Magic Packet aka NTP v2 Monlist Packet
data = "\x17\x00\x03\x2a" + "\x00" * 4
```

---

[5]Ntpdos code retrieved from GitHub at: https://github.com/vpnguy/ntpdos, accessed August 31, 2016.

All the attacker has to do at that point is scan the Internet looking for hosts, most likely unpatched home routers, that are still vulnerable to the monlist command—or return data from any of the remote queries. The attacker can use these hosts to build the redirect list and then launch the attack against the target. To simplify the process even further, an attacker can use a bot-net builder, like Mirai, to scan Internet-accessible home routers and other devices and attempt to connect to those devices using default usernames and passwords. Once successfully connected, the botnet builder will temporarily install the botnet software and ping the command and control server, awaiting instructions on who to attack.

The good news is that more and more Internet Service Providers (ISPs) are taking the threat of NTP-based DDoS attacks seriously and are taking steps to protect their clients, and targets who aren't their clients, from these attacks. NTP DDoS attacks are still very common, but appear to have fallen out of favor as other protocols gain popularity. As ISPs continue to make it harder for attackers to find vulnerable hosts, these attacks will become less common.

However, because of the nature of UDP, NTP will remain a potential source of DDoS attacks. Organizations cannot just rely on their ISPs to fix the problems associated with NTP DDoS attacks—the organization itself must take action to ensure the latest version of NTP is installed on public-facing systems and that secure NTP configurations are deployed throughout the network.

Conclusions

It is easy to read through this chapter and come to the conclusion that NTP is the most insecure program ever written and no one should use it. Nothing could be further from the truth.

Like any program with a 30+ year history, NTP has definitely had major security vulnerabilities over the years. However, the reference code has gotten more secure over the years, and the maintainers of the code have gotten more responsive to fixing reported bugs.

So, while there will undoubtedly continue to be vulnerabilities announced in NTP, it is getting more secure, and major vulnerabilities are becoming less frequent.

Instead, the biggest problem with NTP at this point is with insecure configurations and installations that are never upgraded. The next two chapters will address these issues and offer practical tips for securing NTP.

Securing NTP

This chapter gets to the meat of NTP security: actually securing an NTP installation, and protecting an organization from insecure NTP installations. As previously discussed, this is not always as easy as it sounds, especially given the many platforms in an organization's network that make use of the protocol.

Some platforms, such as Linux or BSD servers, give the administrator a lot more control over the NTP configuration than other systems, such as routers and workstations. Because of this disparity, it is important to understand which systems are making use of NTP and what level of control the administrators have over those systems.

Knowing these two important pieces of information will enable security teams, in conjunction with the various system administrators, to develop a security plan for NTP implementation. It will also help the security team track potential vulnerabilities in the platforms and take appropriate steps to make sure that new vulnerabilities are appropriately prioritized and patched accordingly.

Collecting NTP Information

Unsurprisingly, many organizations have never given NTP security a thought. Unless an organization has been the victim of an NTP Distributed Denial of Service (DDoS) attack, been used as a redirector in one of those attacks, or had an attacker gain access to their network through an NTP vulnerability, there probably has not been much reason to think specifically about NTP security. This means that NTP security may not even be part of an organization's security plan.

© Allan Liska 2016

A. Liska, *NTP Security*, DOI 10.1007/978-1-4842-2412-0_4

Often, NTP is thought of as simply an administrative protocol, and very little consideration is given to NTP security. In fact, in many platforms, there are no options for administrators to add security enhancements to the built-in NTP facility.

For example, most home routers and other so-called Internet of Things (IoT) devices offer limited or no ability to configure NTP settings, at least through the Graphical User Interface (GUI). Some of these devices do offer more control through the command line, but most users are unaware of how to access the command line for these devices.

Apple desktops have ported the reference version of NTP to their platform, offering full configuration options. Microsoft does offer a command line Windows Time client, called w32tm, that enables some of the features of the reference NTP implementation, but not all.

Most organizations opt to simply set the reference clocks through the respective GUI interfaces and leave it at that. Though, for Microsoft Windows desktops connected to a domain controller (DC), the reference clock is the DC and it is set automatically.

This policy makes sense from a security perspective. In fact, in an Active Directory environment that contains a mix of Microsoft Windows and Apple OS X end points, both platforms can use the DC as their NTP server. This keeps the majority of NTP traffic within the network and allows administrators, working with the security team, to set a security policy around NTP connections at a single source.

Forcing desktop systems to connect to an internal domain controller also makes the process of isolating rogue NTP traffic in the network easier. If the majority of hosts in the network are connected to a known internal NTP host, then there should be very little NTP traffic leaving the network.

Remember, maintaining accurate time is important for many types of network communications. So, a lot of connected devices automatically try to connect to pre-configured NTP servers (using pool.ntp.org or other well-known NTP addresses). This, along with the fact that most organizations allow NTP requests to flow out of their network with little interference, means that there may be a large number of potential security risks on the network of which no one is aware.

However, this also allows security analysts to learn what devices on the network are connecting to NTP servers that are not in direct control of the organization. Not only does this give security teams the opportunity to identify potential security risks associated with poor NTP configurations, but it also may identify rogue systems on the network.

The easiest way to understand what type of NTP traffic is attempting to leave an organization's network is to simply set a firewall rule monitoring for any traffic on UDP port 123 (NTP does not have a fallback mechanism to TCP port 123 the way some other UDP protocols do). Any traffic to an unauthorized NTP server should be flagged and investigated.

Note In an ideal security world, the best way to do this would be to block all NTP traffic at the edge of the network which does not originate from stratum 2 NTP servers within the organization and alert on blocked traffic. This would still have the benefit of identifying rogue NTP traffic while simultaneously significantly reducing the risk of an NTP attack. However, the ideal security solution is not always politically practical.

Of course, not all hosts identified using this method will be rogue. Most of them will be servers that were set up long before an NTP security policy was put in place. But this will be a good place to start cataloguing those systems who do not conform to the policy and, hopefully, putting a plan in place to bring them into compliance.

The first thing that needs to be done, especially with older systems that are running vulnerable versions of NTP, is point those hosts to an internal NTP server. If the servers cannot be immediately upgraded, this will at least keep the NTP communication within the network. As outlined in Chapter 3, this will not stop an advanced attacker, but it does limit the damage from more commonplace and less sophisticated attacks.

Secondly, a plan needs to be put in place to upgrade vulnerable NTP servers. Systems that have vulnerabilities which would potentially allow an attacker to gain remote access should be prioritized, especially if those systems are public facing.

Finally, once the organization has identified and upgraded these systems, the next step is to keep up with any updates to the NTP daemon on the systems. Using a Governance, Risk, and Compliance (GRC) solution like RSA's Archer or Lockpath's GRC solution will allow organizations to track the version of different packages (not just NTP) on those systems. Marrying the GRC data with updated vulnerability data from a company like Qualys or Rapid7 will allow an organization to know what is currently installed on their system and access information about new vulnerabilities against NTP on those systems.

Having both sets of intelligence allows organizations to prioritize patching new systems as new NTP vulnerabilities are uncovered. If patching is not possible in a timely manner, knowing that the vulnerability is out there will allow security teams to take additional steps to secure those unpatched systems.

So far, this discussion has revolved around identifying and securing existing systems with NTP installed. But modern organizations are generally much more dynamic, which means new systems are connecting to the network all the time. How should those new systems be secured?

That is the point of adding a section on NTP security to the existing security plan. An NTP security plan allows the security team, in conjunction with the system administrators, to set a base set of guidelines around NTP that a new system must meet in order to connect to the organization's network.

As with any security plan, an NTP security plan does not have to be one size fits all. There may very well be different standards for desktops versus servers, and there will undoubtedly be a different set of rules for internal systems compared to those that are Internet-facing.

A security plan should be flexible enough to allow it to meet the business needs of the organization, while still protecting the organization from known and unknown threats around NTP.

The first step in putting together a plan is to talk about how to harden a server running NTP.

Hardening an NTP Installation

This will sound obvious, but the most effective way to secure an NTP installation is to make sure that it is fully patched, running the latest version of the software.

But that is not always possible. Often NTP is running on closed systems that don't allow administrators to update individual components. Even when it is possible to update individual components, it is not always easy.

For example, as of this writing, the Ubuntu Linux distribution version 16.0.4—one of the most popular distributions—delivers an NTP package with version 4.2.8p4 as the most current version. The most current, non-developer version of NTP is 4.2.8p8, meaning that system administrators relying on Ubuntu package developers for the most recent version of NTP are several iterations behind, and will remain that way.

Even worse is version 14.0.4.5 of Ubuntu, which is not expected to reach end of life (EOL) until April of 2019. That version of the distribution includes version 4.2.6p5 of NTP, which is not only several releases behind the current version, but also includes a number of vulnerabilities that could allow an attacker remote access to the system.

Note The intent here is not to pick on the developers of Ubuntu, who have one of the best Linux distributions available. It doesn't matter which Linux distribution is being discussed—any operating system that relies on a package manager for delivery of updates is going to lag behind the developers of NTP (and other packages) in delivering the most up-to-date applications.

This creates a dilemma for system administrators: run an out-of-date version of NTP or compile and install the most recent NTP package? That may be an easy question to answer for system administrators creating an NTP server, but that is not the most common reason for installing NTP on a server.

If a server is being built to serve primarily as a file server, web server, mail server, or any of hundreds of other functions, NTP is going to be a second-ary service. The administrators will most likely have their hands full with the operation and security of the primary services on the server. NTP mainte-nance (along with any other secondary services) is going to be largely ignored.

There are a number of ways to deal with this. For many organizations, the answer is to build custom images that have the most up-to-date versions of the applications that are running in their environment. Any newly provisioned servers are built on this image and updated appropriately. This way, when new versions of these programs come out, they can be quickly tested and added to the "gold image."

This method keeps the organization up to date with the latest versions of applications used in their environment. Even existing servers can be wiped and rebuilt using an updated image whenever a new gold image is released. This type of maintenance was extremely difficult in environments that relied on physical servers, but as more organizations are moving to virtual servers, it is easier to maintain, update, and test gold images across different teams and applications in the organization.

Other organizations lack the resources to maintain a gold image, and are forced to rely on their chosen Linux distribution to provide updates. Many times, these organizations are unaware that there may be a security risk in this method.

In the second case, it is important to take steps to secure the NTP installation as much as possible. This starts with running NTP in a chroot jail.

Running NTP in a Chroot Jail

Chroot is a Unix process that changes the root directory of a process to one designated by the system administrator. The process, and its children, see the new directory as root and cannot access other files or programs outside of that directory.

The idea here is that even if an attacker is able to use a vulnerability in NTP to gain root access to the server, all that attacker will have access to is the NTP daemon and its child processes. The chroot jail is often used to isolate a program that poses a potential security risk, but needs to run on the system.

Warning The chroot jail is not a security panacea. A skilled enough attacker can break out of a chroot jail, so it should never be the ONLY security step enabled. Instead, the chroot jail should be one of several security steps.

Fortunately, NTP has a built-in facility for running chroot jail (assuming it is compiled with this facility). The command to enable a chroot jail is:

```
allan@server:~# ntpd -i [chroot jail directory] -u [user:group that NTP will run as]
```

This is an example of a basic implementation of the command:

```
allan@server:~# ntpd -i /chroot/usr/sbin/ntpd -u ntp:ntp
```

The NTP daemon must be compiled with the following flags in order to run the NTP daemon in a chroot jail:

- enable-clockctl
- enable-linuxcaps
- enable-solarisprivs

In order for NTP to run in a chroot jail, the operating system must allow NTP to run as a non-root user. This is why the second example above includes the ntp:ntp user:group combination. Running a process as root in a chroot jail defeats the purpose of the jail. A root user can easily break the jailed directory structure and access the rest of the system.

Run NTP As an Unprivileged User

Even when not running in a chroot jail, NTP (and other services) should never be run as root. Always create a user for each service and only give that user the permissions needed to run the service. Anything more than that creates an unnecessary security risk.

This risk is most apparent in attacks that may allow remote access, whether those are buffer overflow attacks or attacks that allow an attacker to execute a remote command. If the NTP daemon is running as root, the attacker will be able to run any command as root once access is gained. By creating a user for NTP with limited permissions and no shell access even if an attacker does gain access to the server the damage they can do will be limited, like this from an Ubuntu /etc/passwd file:

```
ntp:x:105:112::/etc/ntp:/bin/false
```

Some system administrators also use /bin/nologin to accomplish the same thing. The difference between /bin/false and /bin/nologin is that the nologin tag presents a message letting the user know that they are not allowed to log in to the system, whereas the false flag just immediately disconnects. Some security professionals consider the latter more secure, as it does not provide an affirmation that the user exists. This limits the ability of an attacker who does gain access to execute any commands on the system. This is often called the Principle of Least Privilege (POLP). POLP states that a user should have the access needed to perform its required tasks, but no more than that.

While securing the NTP daemon is important, as is restricting unauthorized access, most of the NTP attacks discussed in this book have involved communication. The next step in securing NTP is to secure communication to and from the NTP hosts in the network.

Protecting NTP Communication

Protecting NTP communication does not start at the server—it starts at the edge of an organization's network. For most organizations, there is no reason to run a publicly accessible NTP server. Therefore, blocking all inbound traffic to UDP port 123 is a good place to start.

It is certainly reasonable to maintain a centralized NTP infrastructure for use by systems on the network—in fact, this is an excellent security practice. In an ideal world, organizations would maintain a stratum 1 NTP server in a core data center with stratum 2 servers spread throughout the network. This allows all NTP communication to stay within the network. It also means that an organization can block all incoming and outgoing NTP traffic at the edge firewalls. There would never be a need for any NTP traffic to enter or leave the network.

None of the NTP servers on the network should be receiving requests from external networks. NTP traffic can easily be tunneled through VPNs for remote employees, and for office-to-office traffic NTP communication can be routed over a Multiprotocol Label Switching (MPLS) network that never touches the public Internet. This type of setup improves the NTP security of the network and reduces the risk to an organization that its NTP servers will be used as redirectors in an NTP DDoS attack.

For most organizations, this type of infrastructure is simply not feasible. Managing a stratum 1 NTP server is an ongoing process that requires a level of expertise that is not always available. It also requires additional time and employee resources, which are always in short supply.

A much more likely scenario is for an organization to maintain a number of stratum 2 servers on the network, usually in a peered relationship. These servers are able to reach out to select stratum 1 servers. Or, ideally, one or two stratum 2 servers in the network can reach out to stratum 1 servers. These NTP servers, again in a peering relationship, then become the reference clocks for the other servers in the network, meaning that an organization, depending on its size, may maintain both stratum 2 and stratum 3 servers.

This scenario is significantly less resource intensive and, with modern systems, will not result in significant time drift. It also has the benefit of being easy to secure. The same rules as the first scenario still apply: NTP systems within the organization never need to connect to external NTP servers, and no external servers need to call in to the network. The difference in this case is that the original "deny all in and out on UDP port 123" rule has to be modified. The IP addresses/domain names of the two stratum 2 NTP servers should be allowed to call out to specific stratum 1 NTP servers (not to pool.ntp.org, time.apple.com, or any of the myriad NTP services). For redundancy purposes, at least four stratum 1 servers should be listed in each configuration. All other NTP traffic, in and out of the network, should be blocked.

This does create some additional administrative work. Stratum 1 NTP servers are listed that way in part because of their reliability, not just in terms of their directly connected time source, but also because of their uptime. However, servers are retired, and IP addresses and domains change over time. When selecting a stratum 1 time source, try to identify sources that offer a mailing list or, at the very least, a website that provides regular updates on the status of that NTP server. Appropriate teams within the organization should know when one of the stratum 1 NTP servers is making changes that require configuration updates. Losing one or two stratum 1 servers from the rotation won't impact the reliability of the stratum 2 servers inside the network, but if they aren't replaced, eventually all of the stratum 1 servers could become unreachable. If that were to happen, it would obviously have a significant impact on the ability of the organization to synchronize time.

Conversely, the stratum 2 servers inside the network should be monitored and alerts should be generated when one of the stratum 1 servers is unreachable for a significant amount of time. These types of alerts should be threshold based (the next section will cover this in more detail). Because NTP communication is carried out using UDP, the connections are inherently unreliable. Alerting every time a stratum 1 server is unresponsive would be a waste of time for the team that has to monitor those alerts. Instead, alerts should be generated if a stratum 1 server is unreachable for hours, or even days.

▓ **Note**   Keep in mind that stratum 1 severs are considered Internet infrastructure, and are often targeted for attack in the same way that the root DNS servers are, but unlike the root DNS servers, most stratum 1 servers don't have significant DDoS protections in place. It is possible for a stratum 1 server to be down for days as it experiences an extended DDoS attack and return to service when the attack has ended.

Of course, even if an organization manages to prevent external traffic from reaching NTP servers in the network, that doesn't mean steps shouldn't be taken to secure the NTP servers inside the network. Hardening the server itself, as discussed earlier, is one step. The second step is securing the configuration.

Securing the ntp.conf File

Even in well-secured networks, it is important to maintain a secure NTP configuration, which is primarily done through the ntp.conf file. There are a number of configuration points within the ntp.conf file that can be adjusted to improve security.

Most of the security settings are found in the Access Control section of the ntp.conf file. The access control commands allow NTP server administrators to restrict access to certain requests from remote hosts. A typical set of secure restrictions look like this:

```
restrict -4 default limited kod notrap nomodify nopeer noquery version
restrict -6 default limited kod notrap nomodify nopeer noquery version
```

The first line lists restrictions for incoming IPv4 requests, and the second line lists restrictions for IPv6 requests. This is what each of the restrict commands does:

- Default – Make this the default policy. Any hosts that are allowed to make these queries will need a separate allow statement.

- Limited – Tell the NTP daemon to deny requests from hosts that are in violation of the discard policy set separately (note: this command does nothing if the discard access control is not configured).

- Kod – Send a kiss of death (KoD) packet to any hosts that are in violation of the discard policy (the kod flag requires both a discard access control policy and the limited flag to be set).

- Notrap – Do not send mode 6 control message trap message service responses to requesting hosts.

- Nomodify – Do not allow any remote host to modify the NTP configuration.

- Nopeer – Deny any packets that attempt to set up a peering or other types of association, unless those packets are authenticated.

- Noquery – Deny any queries not specifically related to time service. This is to prevent some of the DDoS tricks discussed in Chapter 3. This flag helps to prevent attacks using the monlist query, as well as other attacks.

- Version – Deny packets that have a different version of NTP set in the packet header. This works well in a closed network that has standardized on NTPv4. There shouldn't be any stray NTPv3 or NTPv2 hosts hiding on the network—if there are, they should not be allowed to synchronize with the NTP server.

The discard command allows NTP administrators to set a minimum and average number of incoming packets from a host before the NTP server starts to limit the server. Both minimum and average values are represented in log2 format (factor of 2). A sample discard line looks like this:

```
discard average 3 minimum 1
```

This line discards packets from any host that has sent packet requests on average every eight seconds, with at least some of the packets being two seconds apart.

The restrict command can also be used as an Access Control List (ACL), only allowing internal hosts to make queries, as in Listing 4-1.

Listing 4-1. Creating an ACL in NTP

```
restrict 127.0.0.1
restrict -6 ::1
restrict [Internal Network/24]
```

Using the restrict command in this manner allows organizations to limit queries to NTP servers from only trusted hosts.

Note The big caveat here, and the reason that ACLs within the ntp.conf file should not be the primary method of restriction, is that NTP packets can be easily forged to either attack an NTP host or use it as a redirector. That is why, whenever possible, ACL restrictions should be in the firewall, not the NTP server.

Secure Configurations on Juniper and Cisco

Both Juniper and Cisco make it easy to secure their NTP configuration. Neither Juniper nor Cisco maintain a reference implementation of NTP, meaning they don't fully support all the features that the NTP daemon on a Linux or UNIX system does.

Because of that, network administrators can simplify their NTP security profile by putting both platforms in client-only mode. In client-only mode, the NTP daemon on the platform will update from a selected server, or servers, but will not respond to remote queries. Whenever possible, it makes sense to configure routers in this manner, using a fully functioning NTP server as the main time synchronization device, which will allow for more robust security.

The process to configure Juniper to be an NTP client is shown in Listing 4-2.

Listing 4-2. Configuring an NTP client on a Juniper router

```
system {
    ntp {
        server [Server IP Address]
        boot-server [Address]
        [optional] authentication-key [key-id] type md5 value
        "[pass-phrase]";
        trusted-key [key-id];
            }
}
```

Configuring a Cisco router to be an NTP client is just as simple, shown in Listing 4-3.

Listing 4-3. Confguring an NTP client on a Cisco router

```
conf t
ntp server [IP Address]
```

Both Juniper and Cisco also support symmetric authentication, which will be discussed in Chapter 5, but neither support AutoKey.

Monitoring NTP Traffic

While NTP is a relatively noisy protocol, it actually generates very little log traffic by default. A typical NTP log will look something like what is shown in Listing 4-4.

Listing 4-4. NTP logs

```
Aug 14 18:47:51 server ntpd[1001]: proto: precision = 0.277 usec
Aug 14 18:47:51 server ntpd[1001]: ntp_io: estimated max descriptors: 1024,
initial socket boundary: 16
Aug 14 18:47:51 server ntpd[1001]: Listen and drop on 0 v4wildcard 0.0.0.0
UDP 123
Aug 14 18:47:51 server ntpd[1001]: Listen and drop on 1 v6wildcard :: UDP
123
Aug 14 18:47:51 server ntpd[1001]: Listen normally on 2 lo 127.0.0.1 UDP 123
Aug 14 18:47:51 server ntpd[1001]: Listen normally on 4 lo ::1 UDP 123
Aug 14 18:47:51 server ntpd[1001]: peers refreshed
```

Not a lot of security-related information is generated via NTP logging. However, NTP also includes the capability to send additional log data using the logconfig command in the ntp.conf file.

The logconfig command consists of four logging classes:

- clock

- peer

- sys

- sync

Each class can be paired with a different logging level depending on the need of the organization. There are four event levels to go with the logging classes:

- info

- events

- statistics

- status

To create the proper logging level, combine the logging class with the logging level to create a single word, such as clockstatus or sysinfo. If an organization wants to log all event classes, the word "all" can be appended to the logging class. So, to maximize the logs collected by the NTP server, the following line could be added to the ntp.conf file:

```
logconfig =clockall +peerall +sysall +syncall
```

Or, this can be simplified to just:

```
logconfig =all
```

In addition to the logging facility, NTP maintains a number of optional stats files. Unfortunately, the data in the stats files is not sent to a centralized logging facility, like syslog, so it has to be examined manually. NTP is able to keep stats on the following information:

- clockstats

- cryptostats

- loopstats

- peerstats

- rawstats

- sysstats

While most of the stats files contain interesting data, they generally do not contain anything of security value. The sysstats file, on the other hand, can contain potentially valuable security information. The output of a typical systats file is shown in Listing 4-5.

Listing 4-5. *Output of a systats file*

```
57646 67671.210 3600 412704 6 351942 60762 1 0 39 0 18209 8871575
57646 71271.210 3600 576690 5 440408 136282 1 0 103 0 37207 8882021
57646 74871.210 3600 661329 5 489401 171927 2 2 267 0 59467 8897683
57646 78471.210 3600 583562 4 445575 137984 7 0 75 0 54384 8908898
57646 82071.210 3600 673489 5 495913 177576 0 0 268 0 57170 8922985
57646 85671.210 3600 655043 6 482748 172295 2 0 157 0 57531 8936466
```

What might initially look like gibberish actually contains potentially valuable security information, once the fields are properly processed. To better understand the fields, take a look at the last line:

```
57646 85671.210 3600 655043 6 482748 172295 2 0 157 0 57531 8936466
```

The first two fields are the date and the time (in seconds and fractions of a second). The third field is the time, in hours, since the server was last rebooted. The fourth field, 655043, is the number of packets received. The fifth field is the number of packets processed. The sixth field, 482748, is the number of NTP requests that matched the current NTP version, while the seventh field, 172295, is the number of NTP requests that matched the previous NTP version. The eighth field, 2, is the number of incoming NTP requests that contain a version of NTP that is no longer supported.

The ninth field, 0, is the number of denied requests. The 10th field, 157, is the number of incoming requests that had a bad length or format. The 11th field, 0, contains the number of packets that had bad authentication. Field 12 is the number of packets discarded due to rate limitation. The final field contains the number of KoD packets sent to persistent hosts. The final field will not be there if KoD has not been configured.

Because each line in the sysstats file represents an hour's worth of statistical information, there is a lot of potential security value that can be gleaned by hunting through the files. For example, notice the number of requests is fairly steady hour to hour. If there is a sudden spike in the number of requests, that may indicate that the NTP server is being used as a redirector for a DDoS attack. Similarly, in a homogenous network that has standardized on NTP version 4, seeing a number of NTP version 3 or bad version requests to the server may indicate the server is being probed, or someone has already launched an attack on the server.

While the data in the sysstats file may be very useful for detecting anomalous events and initiating a security investigation, it doesn't do the security team any good if the file is unreachable. Syslog events are limited, but have the advantage that they can be forwarded to a centralized server for monitoring and analysis. In order to take advantage of the data in the sysstats file, there has to be a way to alert on it.

Alerting on NTP Security Issues

Logging is not very useful if there isn't corresponding alerting on the logs being generated. Syslog has the benefit of allowing security teams to create rules, especially in a Security Information and Event Manager (SIEM). Sending NTP logs to the SIEM allows security teams to write rules that will alert on things like an NTP daemon restarting, de-peering with one of its peers, or attempting to make a large clock adjustment. All of these are potential signs of attack.

Some of the more advanced SIEMs can even process unstructured data, like that in the sysstats file, and allow security teams to create alert thresholds based on behavior that is odd for that particular NTP server.

But the NTP server simply does not provide enough information in its logs or stats to determine whether or not an attacker is really targeting the server. Instead, in order to alert with confidence, the logs and statistics from the NTP server must be correlated with other security tools.

Correlating Alerts

Firewall rules were discussed earlier in this chapter, and they make a good correlation point with the server logs. If suspicious activity occurs over UDP port 123 on the firewall and a few minutes later suspicious activity occurs on the NTP server itself, the security team now has a clearer picture of what the attack looks like. Of course, these two log sources leave out an important bit of context: the content of the attack.

That is why Intrusion Detection/Prevention System (IDS/IPS) logs should be added to the mix. The Talos team at Cisco, which now maintains the snort community signature base, has developed a number of signatures that detect malicious NTP behavior. See Listing 4-6.

Listing 4-6. Two snort signatures to detect malicious NTP traffic

```
# alert udp $EXTERNAL_NET any -> $HOME_NET 123 (msg:"DELETED EXPLOIT ntpdx
overflow attempt"; flow:to_server; dsize:>128; reference:arachnids,492;
reference:bugtraq,2540; reference:cve,2001-0414; reference:nessus,10647;
classtype:attempted-admin; sid:312; rev:9;)

# alert udp $EXTERNAL_NET any -> $HOME_NET 123 (msg:"SERVER-OTHER ntp
monlist denial of service attempt"; flow:to_server; content:"|17 00 03
2A|"; depth:4; detection_filter:track by_dst, count 1000, seconds 5;
metadata:service ntp; reference:cve,2013-5211; classtype:attempted-dos;
sid:29393; rev:3;)
```

The first rule detects an older buffer overflow attack against NTP, while the second rule is looking for monlist activity. Both of these rules provide context to the alerts being generated by the other devices. By correlating NTP server and router logs with firewall and IDS/IPS alerts in a centralized location, the security team can not only be alerted, but also have a great deal of context around the attack and whether or not it was successful. That allows the security team to effectively prioritize the alerts and respond appropriately.

Conclusions

NTP security is not just about securing the NTP installation itself. Rather, NTP security really involves multiple systems and groups within an organization. For an effective NTP security plan, the security team has to work with system and network administrators to get their support and implement a standard NTP deployment across the network.

Before any of this can be done, an organization must take stock of the network and learn which systems on the network are running NTP, which version of NTP they are running, and which NTP servers on the Internet these systems are using.

Once all of that information is in place, an NTP security plan can be put together with the goal of helping the organization improve security, without inconveniencing the workforce.

Once the plan is in place, it is important to monitor security systems within the organization to ensure that new devices that come online stay compliant to the new policy and that the infrastructure stays up and running.

This process includes incorporating NTP monitoring into the existing monitoring system and knowing what to look for in NTP alerts. It also means being able to correlate NTP logs with the firewall, IDS/IPS logs, and any security system that touches the NTP protocol.

Securing NTP Infrastructure

NTP security is not just a matter of protecting the infrastructure—it is also requires making sure that infrastructure has a high level of availability. Availability is especially important for those organizations that choose to run their own NTP infrastructure rather than use publicly available NTP servers.

One of the most important features of NTP is that it is designed to be robust and redundant. This resiliency is part of the reason why the protocol has out-lived many of the competing standards that have developed over the years.

Unfortunately, when operating NTP in a closed environment, it may become necessary to replicate that robustness on a much smaller scale. Fortunately, NTP offers a number of options that allow organizations to deploy a robust NTP infrastructure without a lot of capital expenditure.

On top of a redundant infrastructure, there are steps that organizations can take within their infrastructure to limit or eliminate the potential damage caused by NTP-based Distributed Denial of Service (DDoS) attacks.

BCP38

As discussed in several places in this book, one of NTP's biggest security threats is NTP traffic being used in DDoS attacks. As a protocol, UDP is trivi-ally easy to forge. This means that attackers can send large amounts of NTP traffic from victim NTP hosts to targeted servers by making those victims think that the original request came from those targeted servers.

© Allan Liska 2016
A. Liska, *NTP Security*, DOI 10.1007/978-1-4842-2412-0_5

That is where Best Current Practice 38 (BCP38) comes in. BCP38 is outlined in RFC 3704, which describes ways in which operators can configure their network infrastructure to deny spoofed packets the ability to traverse the network and ensure that all network traffic can be traced back to its actual original network.

Originally, this type of configuration was not implemented on edge networks, but primarily used on transit networks. However, organizations have begun adopting BCP38 on edge networks as a way to prevent their organization from being used to redirect DDoS attacks to other networks and as a low-cost way to keep bad traffic from targeting their network.

In addition, to the standard amplification DDoS attacks, BCP38 can be used to help prevent NTP broadcast attacks, which is another type of NTP DDoS attack.

■ **Note**   More information, and the most up-to-date information, about BCP38 is available at www.bcp38.info.

Broadcast Attacks

Chapter 1 discussed the option of configuring NTP in broadcast mode. Broadcast mode flips the client-to-server model that NTP normally uses, and instead the NTP server broadcasts the time to an entire network. The clients, also configured to listen in broadcast mode, pick up the time from the NTP server and, as long as the origin timestamp from the server is correct, it will update its time.

This is the way it is supposed to work in theory, but there are some problems with the way broadcast mode is implemented, as documented in an NTP bug and patched in version 4.2.8p6, which could allow an attacker to disrupt time on an entire broadcast network.

As a refresher, when NTP is configured in broadcast mode, the NTP administrator adds a line like this to the NTP configuration file:

```
broadcast 10.100.255.255
```

In Chapter 1, the same example used a smaller Class C network block, but the broadcast command is not limited to just Class C network blocks—any size network block will work.

In this particular case, the NTP server is sending NTP updates to all hosts in the 10.100.0.0/16 netblock. When the host sends out its request, it does so in Mode 5, which is the broadcast server mode. When the clients are negotiating broadcast mode, they will send responses in Mode 6, the client broadcast mode. After that, they will listen for updates.

But if an attacker sent a legitimate time query to one of the clients on the network their reply will include the IP address of the broadcast server. Now an attacker can send a spoofed broadcast packet with bad data that appears to come from the legitimate broadcast server. The broadcast server will also be sending out legitimate updates while the attacker is carrying out the attack. This will create confusion among the NTP clients on the network, and they will eventually disassociate themselves from the broadcast server, severing the relationship and causing a disruption in time services.

BCP38 is one way to defeat this type of attack as well as other NTP-based DDoS attacks.

Implementing BCP38

BCP38 is not a special command on a router or firewall, but rather a series of access control lists (ACLs) that Internet engineers at the Internet Engineering Task Force (IETF) recommend putting in place, after a lot of testing, to ensure that the traffic leaving an organization's network or traversing across an Internet provider's backbone is only allowed to do so if the source IP address matches the network origin of that IP address.

This means that the configuration is going to vary from network to network, but the implementation is going to be the same. There are at least five ways that BCP38 can be implemented in a network:

1. ingress access lists

2. Strict Reverse Path Forwarding

3. Feasible Path Reverse Path Forwarding

4. Loose Reverse Path Forwarding

5. Loose Reverse Path Forwarding ignoring default routes

The simplest method of implementing BCP38 is by using ingress access lists. Ingress access lists are designed for smaller, largely static networks. Setting up an ingress access list involves gathering all networks that are owned by the organization. Network administrators then create ACLs that don't allow any traffic that does not have a source address from one of those networks to leave the network. In other words, the organization prevents any potentially spoofed traffic from ever jumping from their network to that of their upstream provider or to the target of the attack.

Note Any and all of the solutions for BCP38 should include preventing any traffic with a source address from a reserved netblock, the so-called RFC1918 IP address space, from leaving the network. Reserved IP address space are network blocks that are meant to be used as internal IP addresses and never routed across the Internet. Those addresses include 10.0.0.0 - 10.255.255.255; 172.16.0.0 - 172.31.255.255; and 192.168.0.0 - 192.168.255.255.

Of course, in a dynamic organization with constantly changing network allocations, the ingress access list solution can be a challenge to manage, and it does not scale for really large organizations or transit providers.

An alternative to ingress access lists is Strict Reverse Path Forwarding (SRPF). The concept behind SRPF is similar to that of ingress access lists, but instead of using static ACLs, SRPF uses dynamic access lists.

Under SRPF, the source IP address of every packet is looked up in the Forwarding Information Base (FIB) to see if the incoming packet is on the interface that would be used to forward a responding packet. If the packet is considered good, it is then forwarded to the next hop—otherwise, it is dropped. For example, if an NTP packet hits the edge router with a source IP address of 208.12.34.82, the router will query the FIB and determine if its routing tables would normally forward packets with that destination IP address along that same interface. If the answer is yes, the packet is sent to the next hop.

Unsurprisingly, this additional lookup does increase the load on the router, especially compared to the simpler ingress access list model. What is surprising is that the load increase is not always that significant. Obviously, something like SRPF should be thoroughly tested in a lab environment before being deployed. But many organizations have seen success with SRPF, without having to sacrifice network performance.

Both ingress access lists and SRPF run into a problem in multi-homed environments where there may be multiple paths that a packet can take to reach its final destination. This type of asymmetric routing is common in large enterprises and transit networks that have more than one connection or use the Border Gateway Protocol (BGP) to manage routing.

In cases like that, organizations can use Feasible Path Reverse Path Forwarding (FRPF). FRPF works the same way as SRPF, except the FIB returns multiple paths for an incoming source IP address. The router ensures that the interface on which a packet arrives is one of many possible paths for return traffic of the source IP address.

This allows for better control in large networks, and while it may result in some malicious traffic being improperly routed, it still cuts down on most malicious activity.

Loose Reverse Path Forwarding (LRPF) is rarely used, except in the largest transit providers. LRPF works like SRPF and FRPF, except that it only checks to see if there is a feasible route to a source IP address. In other words, if there is a return path to the source IP address of an incoming packet on any of the router's interfaces, the router will send the packet to the next hop. LRPF is primarily useful for weeding out incoming packets that have an RFC1918 source IP address. Those addresses are not commonly used in DoS or DDoS attacks, especially not in amplification-style DDoS attacks. So, while LRPF does provide some level of protection, it is not fully adequate to stop DDoS attacks.

The final option, LRPF ignoring default routes, is LRPF that gives priority to default routes. So, if a source IP address is looked up in the FIB and a router sees there is no route in the FIB but there is a default route to the IP address, that default route is given precedent and the packet is forwarded on to its destination. LRPF ignoring default routes is primarily used at exchanges, where one transit provider peers with one or more other transit providers to pass traffic.

BCP38 is a potentially powerful tool that can be used to add a layer of protection to an organization without additional cost. A network or security team can query an organization's upstream ISP about whether or not it has implemented BCP38 as part of the security plan that has to do with NTP.

Though BCP38 does not just impact NTP, it really is a protection against any sort of DoS or DDoS attack that uses a UDP-based protocol as part of the attack.

NTP Pooling

BCP38 provides a way to secure an organization from a DDoS attack, and also prevent the organization from being used to launch a DDoS attack. But BCP38 does not help to improve the resiliency of an internally hosted NTP infrastructure. One way to improve the robustness of an NTP infrastructure is to use the NTP pooling facility.

To this point in the book, whenever the discussion has revolved around adding NTP servers to the configuration file, the server command has always been used, as in Listing 5-1.

Listing 5-1. Listing NTP servers in the ntp.conf file

```
server [Server 1]
server [Server 2]
server [Server 3]
server [Server 4]
```

There are other commands that can be used to add servers, in this case the pool command, as shown in Listing 5-2.

Listing 5-2. A list of pool servers in the ntp.conf file

```
pool 0.pool.ntp.org
pool 1.pool.ntp.org
pool 2.pool.ntp.org
pool 3.pool.ntp.org
```

At first glance, the commands don't look all that different, but the underlying capability is very different. The server command is designed to define static, unchanging servers, almost always using IP addresses, whereas the pool command is more dynamic. NTP uses DNS to update the servers it is reaching out to, rotating through many more servers more often.

The example above uses the most well-known NTP pool addresses—pool.ntp.org—but the process works for any domain as long as the DNS back end is set up properly.

Using pool addresses allows a large organization to maintain a number of servers running NTP as a secondary service and distribute the traffic to those services evenly. NTP already uses a number of "foot race" algorithms designed to distribute the load between the NTP servers listed in the configuration file, to ensure that no one server sees the bulk of the traffic. By switching to pool addresses, that distribution effect can be multiplied.

The way this works is that an organization identifies a number of servers in the network that are going to also serve as NTP servers. They can be mail servers, file servers, web servers, even routers and switches. These machines will all synchronize with stratum 1 servers, either on network or off.

Each of the newly identified servers will be clustered into one of the pool addresses. Using the format from the example above, an organization might have a DNS record that looks like Listing 5-3.

Listing 5-3. DNS listing for 0.ntp.example.com

```
allan:~ allan$ dig 0.ntp.example.com
0.ntp.example.com.          150     IN    A     10.100.152.87
0.ntp.example.com.          150     IN    A     10.100.5.32
0.ntp.example.com.          150     IN    A     192.168.7.45
0.ntp.example.com.          150     IN    A     192.168.23.58
```

Note that querying for 0.ntp.example.com returns four IP addresses, so if there are four pool addresses loaded into the NTP configuration, that means there are actually 16 servers participating in the NTP foot race at any time, meaning each NTP server is seeing a small portion of the NTP traffic.

The second part of the DNS configuration to note is the low Time to Live (TTL) for the A record for 0.ntp.example.com. The TTL is set to 150 seconds, which means that a new set of NTP servers will be sent out every 2.5 minutes. Assuming an organization maintains 0.ntp.example.com, 1.ntp.example.com, 2.ntp.example.com, and 3.ntp.example.com, as in the pool.ntp.org example above, dozens of servers could be masked behind each of those addresses and the rotation would ensure that no one server ever experienced a significant load while keeping a robust infrastructure in place, allowing the organization to deliver effective NTP service at a low cost both in terms of resource utilization and expenditure.

The pool.ntp.org has more than 3800 servers participating in their pool project as of October 2016. Each one of those servers receives millions of connections each day, with no disruption in the overall service. Creating an NTP pool can be a very cost-effective way for a large organization to deliver a robust NTP infrastructure.

NTP Over Multicast/Manycast

Another way to provide redundant NTP infrastructure is to use either multicast or manycast addressing. Both of these services allow NTP clients to discover NTP servers in different ways, but both serve the purpose of somewhat automating the NTP discovery process across an entire network.

Multicast

Multicast is a "one to many" form of communication between hosts on a network. Originally designed as a broadcasting protocol, multicast is used to offer a range of services, including NTP.

The Internet Assigned Numbers Authority (IANA) has reserved two addresses for NTP to be used in multicast addressing. For IPv4 networks, the address is 224.0.1.1, and for IPv6 networks, the address is FF05::101 for site-local and FF08::101 for organization-local. These addresses should only be used in networks where the multicast span is well contained, to avoid leakage into other networks.

In cases where using the reserved multicast address might result in bleeding into other networks, using the multicast addresses defined in RFC 2365 (239.0.0.0-239.255.255.255) is an alternative.

Configuring multicast is very similar to configuring NTP for broadcast mode—in fact, on the server side, it is the same. Simply add the following line to the ntp.conf file:

```
broadcast 224.0.1.1
```

On the client side, the command to enable multicast configuration is multicastclient. Again, the configuration would look similar. Instead of a server or pool statement, the configuration would look like this:

```
multicastclient 224.0.1.1
```

For an additional layer of redundancy, some hosts can be configured as both multicast clients and broadcast servers. Again, this allows an organization to distribute the load of NTP requests across multiple systems.

Given that the security risks in a multicast environment are similar to those of a broadcast environment, symmetric authentication should be used for client and server communication.

Manycast

NTP also supports the use of manycast to create a redundant environment. Manycast was first introduced into NTPv4 and is not the same as the anycast protocol, though NTP can be configured to run over anycast as well.

Manycast allows for automatic discovery of clients and servers on a closed network. It also allows for the clients to make intelligence choices about which servers it is going to use for time synchronization.

A manycast client is configured with the manycastclient command and a broadcast IP address, instead of a server or pool address:

```
manycastclient 192.168.1.255
```

The manycast client only reaches out to the network when it is in need of an update, based on the current minclock and tos stats. When the client sends the update request, it is a normal client mode message, but sent to the broadcast address.

Servers listening to the same broadcast address and that meet the minimum requirements listed in the client mode packet sent out, including being at a lower numbered stratum level (for instance, a stratum 3 server cannot reply to a stratum 3 client), send a unicast response to the client and are added to the NTP server rotation for that client.

As with normal NTP communication, the client engages in the footrace with its current NTP servers until they drop out and the manycast process starts up again.

As with the multicast configuration, manycast clients can also double as servers, allowing organizations to maximize redundancy within their NTP infrastructure. Also, as with multicast and broadcast traffic, manycast should be implemented with proper symmetric key authentication to avoid spoofing attacks.

Conclusions

It is not enough to secure the NTP server and the configuration. System administrators and security teams must also secure NTP communication at the network level. Part of that is ensuring that spoofed NTP packets don't enter or leave the network.

But securing NTP communication also means providing a robust and redundant NTP infrastructure that can be used throughout the network. Using multicast and manycast as ways to create an auto discovery process in the network helps to improve the reliability of an internal NTP infrastructure and, if configured properly, can also help to improve the security of that NTP infrastructure.

When configured properly, an organization can improve their overall NTP security by managing all or most of the infrastructure in-house. If NTP traffic never leaves the organization and outside NTP requests can be dismissed at the edge of the network, then a potential threat to the organization has been removed.

Alternatives to NTP

Given the number of security problems discussed in this book and that have been discovered and published over the years, it is not surprising that some organizations opt to run alternatives to the NTP reference client. There are a number of different options available.

In addition to using alternative code bases, it is also possible to install NTP appliances. Companies like TimeTools, Microsemi, and Galleon Systems provide purpose-built NTP servers. These servers are designed to be stratum 1 servers with direct connections to either GPS or radio clocks, and can provide a source of accurate time and possibly improve the security of an organization's NTP infrastructure.

The challenge with using an appliance vendor is that they may provide limited insight into the code that is running on the appliance. For all of its flaws, the NTP reference code is constantly being reviewed by some of the best security experts in the industry. Before choosing to go with an NTP appliance, it is a good idea to understand what code is running on the server, how that code is maintained, what security precautions are in place, and how often (and how) it is updated. Many NTP appliances simply run the NTP reference code, which is not a bad thing, unless the appliance cannot be easily updated or requires waiting for the vendor to release a patch.

© Allan Liska 2016
A. Liska, *NTP Security*, DOI 10.1007/978-1-4842-2412-0_6

Again, NTP appliances can increase the NTP security of an organization by keeping all NTP traffic internal to the network, but there are potential risks that need to weighed against the benefits of creating an NTP wall within the organization.

Separate from the appliance, there are also a number of different NTP builds that may be worth investigating as alternatives to the NTP reference code.

NTPSec

Probably the most popular alternative to the NTP reference code is NTPSec (www.ntpsec.org). NTPSec is actually built on the NTP reference code, but it has removed many of the most problematic features of NTP.

Overall, the developers of NTPSec claim to have removed more than 140,000 lines of code. This significantly reduces the attack surface of their NTP installation, but it goes deeper than that. The developers behind NTPSec have removed a number of the legacy features from the NTP code that they feel should no longer be supported.

This is the problem with a code base that is almost 30 years old—even the most recent version of NTP is more than 15 years old. The developers of NTP have also tried very hard to maintain backward compatibility with older versions of NTP. This means there is older code and there are older capabilities that someone developing NTP would never deliver today.

The code that has been removed from NTP includes:

- The ntpdc utility—instead, its functionality has been merged into the still-included ntpq utility.

- Not all features of ntpq have been maintained. Commands that were prone to use by attackers, such as the saveconfig command and other commands used to show the running config, have all been removed.

- The NTPSec developers have removed the ntpdate command as well or, more accurately, they have repurposed it as a wrapper around ntpdig, so the functionality is still there.

- Given the complexity and lack of real-world deployment of AutoKey, that has been removed as well.

Overall, the developers have removed 60% of the legacy reference NTP code. At the same time, they have done a thorough review of the code, looking for boundary errors, buffer overflows, and common security bugs that have plagued NTP, to put patches in place and harden the code itself.

By removing unnecessary features and hardening the code, the hope of the developers is to provide an easier-to-use but more secure NTP server that is still compatible with NTP servers around the world.

Because the underlying code is the same, the installation and configuration of the NTPSec daemon is the same. While NTPSec does not include support for AutoKey, it does include support for symmetric key authentication. It also sets a default policy that unauthenticated packets that may consume significant resources, such as broadcast packets, require authentication. This adds a layer of security against broadcast and other types of NTP DDoS attacks.

The NTPSec team has made some great strides in improving the security of the base NTP code. They have also done an important thing by breaking with legacy NTP systems. While the reference code must continue to support outdated versions of NTP, the NTPSec team does not. Being forced to maintain compliance with outdated codebases has caused many security problems over time, not just with NTP, but with a host of other platforms such as DNS, and even software such as Microsoft Windows. Starting fresh and forcing compliance with a more secure code base is a good way to start.

Unfortunately, based on GitHub numbers, it does not look like NTPSec has garnered a lot of attention at this point. Given time and more NTP security announcements, this will most likely change, and more organizations will choose to adopt it and contribute to its success. In the meantime, the development is very active and making constant improvements to the code.

Ntimed

Ntimed (nwtime.org/ntimed) is a completely new NTP daemon, written from scratch and redesigned to operate more efficiently and securely while still operating over UDP port 123 and retaining the ability to communicate with existing NTP infrastructure.

Ntimed is being developed by Poul-Henning Kamp and is funded by the Linux Foundation's Core Infrastructure Initiative. According to Kamp, the reason for completely re-writing NTP rather than trying to fix the reference NTP code is simple:

> "…after studying the 300,000+ lines of source-code in NTPD, I concluded that while it could be salvaged, it would be more economical, much faster and far more efficient to start from scratch."

Ntimed actually breaks down into three different components: ntimed-client, ntimed-slave, and ntimed-master. The ntimed-client sits on hosts and servers and exists only to reach out to upstream NTP servers to get the current time and update the local clock.

The ntimed-slave acts as middleware, serving as a conduit for the ntimed-clients to get updates on time while also getting updated time from the ntimed-masters. The final host type, the ntimed-master, is connected to reference clocks and provides updates to the ntimed-slaves.

This three-tiered system greatly simplifies the layers in a typical NTP chain, and by providing a client-only option, ntimed can help to provide better security for the NTP endpoints.

Ntimed is also unique in that it is not beholden to just NTP. Users will eventually be able to overlay Ntimed on other network time protocols, such as precision time protocol (PTP).

The early releases of Ntimed look promising. The code base is clean and doesn't have some of the problems that the NTP reference daemon does. Setup and configuration have also been simplified. Rather than using a configuration file, everything appears to run from the command line. Ntimed can be downloaded from GitHub (github.com/bsdphk/Ntimed)

However, it is not a full-featured client at this point. Some of the security features in the NTP daemon are not implemented in Ntimed. Most notably, there is no authentication capability at this point. It will most likely be added in the future, but it is not there today.

At this point, Ntimed is a project worth keeping an eye on and testing in a lab environment, but it is not ready for live deployment. Given time, it could become a valuable tool for organizations that want a lightweight and secure way of synchronizing time in their network.

tlsdate

One of the concerns about NTP is that it does not provide a mechanism to encrypt traffic between server and client, or even between peers. Part of the reason for this is the nature of NTP traffic requires it to be encrypted, and part of it is because the maintainers of the NTP reference code want to use as few resources as possible on NTP servers.

Remember, unlike other protocols such as HTTP, SMTP, or DNS, NTP generally does not run on a standalone server. Instead, NTP is run on a server that has a main function. This means that keeping the queries as lightweight as possible is imperative. Even though an encryption extension could be added to the protocol, as DNS has done with DNSSEC, it is not likely to happen in the near future.

For most organizations, that is fine. Generally, organizations that are concerned about this level of security implement a fully redundant NTP infrastructure that exists entirely in their network. It doesn't encrypt the NTP communication, but it does keep non-encrypted traffic from leaving the organization's network.

Other organizations don't have that luxury. This is where tlsdate may fill a niche. Tlsdate is an application that updates local time over a transport layer security (TLS) connection, more commonly referred to as HTTPS. A version of tlsdate is available on GitHub (github.com/ioerror/tlsdate)

Tsdate bypasses the NTP protocol entirely and takes advantage of the fact that that a byproduct of an HTTPS connection to a server is that it provides the client with the current time on that server. Using two functions built in to TLS, ClientHello and ServerHello—both of which provide the date of their respective hosts—tlsdate can synchronize the time of the client to that server.

The date stamp provided by a TLS server is nowhere near as accurate as that provided by NTP, but for many organizations, it may be enough. Using tlsdate would allow an organization to completely disable NTP on all systems and rely on TLS, a protocol that is encrypted and already allowed on almost every network, to manage their time synchronization needs.

That being said, there are some potential downfalls of using this method. The most obvious is that TLS is not designed for this function, and at any point, this method could disappear from future versions of TLS. It is also not as robust as NTP infrastructure—there are not necessarily redundant services in place to support this type of time synchronization. Tlsdate also does not have any functions in place to ensure that the reference clock actually keeps accurate time. Because there is no concept of layers or stratums in tlsdate, the client has to trust that the server has an accurate and updated clock.

Tlsdate is an interesting idea, and if more people implement tlsdate it is possible for the TLS standard to change to support this type of time synchronization (see the current move to deliver DNS requests over HTTP). Until then, it is probably best to play with the concept but not implement it in a production environment.

Precision Time Protocol (PTP)

Rather than try to create updates to software that uses NTP, some developers have created alternatives to NTP, the most well-known being the Precision Time Protocol (PTP). PTP was introduced by the Institute of Electrical and Electronic Engineers (IEEE) in 2002 as IEEE-1588-2002, has been updated with IEEE-1588-2008, and is being updated again as IEEE-1588-2013.

PTP is a time synchronization protocol capable of running in an IPv4 or IPv6 environment that uses UDP ports 319 and 320 for communication. PTP delivers sub-microsecond accuracy in clock timing.

PTP is designed by the IEEE to be lightweight using minimal computing resources and able to run equally well on small microcomputers and large mainframes or industrial systems, and it must do so with minimal traffic. It is extensible, with the ability to communicate over a wide range of mechanisms using whatever available networking infrastructure is in place. It is also designed to be easily managed both locally and remotely.

PTP uses a three-tiered clock system: grandmaster clock, master clock, and slave clock. The grandmaster clock is designed to be the reference clock for the entire network. The master clock gets its time from the grandmaster clock. In turn, the master clock provides time updates for the slave clock.

Unlike NTP, in PTP systems, communication between master and slave clocks is reversed, with the master sending updates to the slave letting them know what the current time is on the master and the slave responding with any delays between the master clock and the slave clock. The process is similar to running NTP in broadcast mode—in fact, broadcast mode is one of the methods of communication for IEEE-1588-2008. Master clocks can receive updates from other master clocks that are not grandmaster clocks. In cases where this happens, the master clock must decide if it wants to remain a master clock or become a slave clock.

With so many similarities between NTP and PTP, why the two different protocols? NTP is designed to work over large, wide area networks on a variety of different systems, while PTP is designed to work in a more controlled network environment on a number of heterogeneous systems. Because of this more controlled environment, it is easier to operate a protocol like PTP that has minimal configuration options and is very lightweight.

There is a Linux-based implementation of PTP on GitHub called ptpd (github.com/ptpd/ptpd) that is available for download and is a full-reference implementation. The ptpd code is well-maintained and kept up to date.

One word of caution about PTP is that it has not currently implemented any security features. Security is a big part of the update to IEEE-1588-2013, so it should be a much more secure protocol once that is complete. However, running PTP as an NTP alternative on an internal network poses minimal security risk, with the caveat that whatever code base is used is carefully reviewed for potential security flaws.

Conclusions

While there are a number of steps that organizations can take to improve the security of their NTP installation, some organizations prefer to use other, more secure clients. Some may even prefer to use different mechanisms for synchronizing time.

While NTP has been the gold standard for 30 years, and the NTP team has made great improvements to NTP (and is continuing to do so), the reference NTP daemon may not be right for every organization. It doesn't hurt to explore some of the alternatives.

That being said, organizations should be wary about falling into some of the traps that NTP fell into several years ago with regard to security. Remember that the NTP code base is constantly being inspected by security researchers around the world, looking for and reporting vulnerabilities. A smaller code base with fewer users may not get the same attention, and serious security flaws could be overlooked. Finding serious security flaws is not necessarily a bad thing—the problem comes when it takes months to get those flaws fixed, or worse, they never get fixed, leaving organizations who have deployed that code vulnerable to attack.

No matter which route your organization chooses, when it comes to network time synchronization, you should make sure the deployment is added to the existing security plan. This will allow the security team to make sure it is tracking for new vulnerabilities in the platform and the protocol, monitoring for changes in best practice for deployment and configuration, and watching out for new exploits in the wild against the platform.

I

Index

© Allan Liska 2016
A. Liska, *NTP Security*, DOI 10.1007/978-1-4842-2412-0

Get the eBook for only $4.99!

Why limit yourself?

Now you can take the weightless companion with you wherever you go and access your content on your PC, phone, tablet, or reader.

Since you've purchased this print book, we are happy to offer you the eBook for just $4.99.

Convenient and fully searchable, the PDF version enables you to easily find and copy code—or perform examples by quickly toggling between instructions and applications.

To learn more, go to http://www.apress.com/us/shop/companion or contact support@apress.com.

Printed in the United States
By Bookmasters